# The Battle for the Black Ballot

LANDMARK LAW CASES
&
AMERICAN SOCIETY

Peter Charles Hoffer
N. E. H. Hull
Williamjames Hull Hoffer
*Series Editors*

For a complete list of titles in the series go to www.kansaspress.ku.edu

CHARLES L. ZELDEN

# The Battle for the Black Ballot

*Smith v. Allwright* and

the Defeat of the Texas

All-White Primary

UNIVERSITY PRESS OF KANSAS

Published by the University Press of Kansas (Lawrence, Kansas 66045), which was organized by the Kansas Board of Regents and is operated and funded by Emporia State University, Fort Hays State University, Kansas State University, Pittsburg State University, the University of Kansas, and Wichita State University

Library of Congress Cataloging-in-Publication Data

Zelden, Charles L. 1963–

The battle for the black ballot : Smith v. Allwright and the defeat of the Texas all-white primary / Charles L. Zelden

p.   cm — (Landmark law cases & American society)

Includes bibliographical references and index.

ISBN 978-0-7006-1340-3 (pbk. : alk. paper)

1. Smith, Lonnie — Trials, litigation, etc.   2. Trials — Texas.   3. African Americans — Suffrage — Texas — History.   4. African Americans — Suffrage— United States — History.   I. Title.   II. Series.

KF228.S553Z45 2004

342.73'072'09764—dc22      2004006075

British Library Cataloguing-in-Publication Data is available.

Printed in the United States of America

10 9 8 7 6 5 4 3 2

The paper used in this publication is recycled and contains 30 percent postconsumer waste. It is acid free and meets the minimum requirements of the American National Standard for Permanence of Paper for Printed Library Materials z39.48–1992.

# CONTENTS

No modern legal historian would deny a proposition that a hundred years ago was anathema to lawyers and judges as well as most scholars: There is no bright-line distinction between law and politics. There is no better proof of this proposition than the long and tangled history of the Texas Democratic Party's all-white primary (AWP), and Charles L. Zelden's powerful story of the rise and fall of the AWP reminds us of the consequences of the proposition.

After Reconstruction had failed, Texas Democrats sought to deny the vote to people of color in the state. Because Texas was a one-party state, the Democratic Party primary effectively determined who would hold office. In 1921, the Supreme Court of the United States had ruled that party primaries were not the kind of state action contemplated by the framers of the Fourteenth Amendment. In effect, the High Court privatized what everyone — at least everyone in Texas — knew was the election process. The state legislature immediately passed a law barring blacks from voting in the primary. In 1927, the Supreme Court struck down this law because the state itself had acted to deny blacks the vote. The state legislature responded by giving to the Democratic Party leadership the power to certify who was and who was not a Democrat for the purposes of voting in the primary. The Court was not fooled by this subterfuge and struck down the new law in 1932.

The Democratic leaders were not going to sit idly by and allow lily white government to fall. They repealed all laws governing the conduct of party primaries, expecting that the Democratic convention would bar black voting, which it did. The Court refused, in 1935, to intervene because, as Justice Owen Roberts opined, political parties were not government agencies and the Fourteenth Amendment could not reach them (just as it could not reach other public but not state-run institutions like movie theaters and amusement parks). But the state had gone too far, and the Court in 1941 upheld congressional regulation of the conduct of primaries. If Congress regarded the primary as a quasi-state activity, so would the High Court. In *Smith v. Allwright*, an eight to one majority of the Court found the AWP unconstitutional. The only dissenter was Justice Roberts.

This short summary of the tug-of-war between the High Court

and the State of Texas omits the massive research and great drama of Zelden's account. Using local as well as state and federal records, and adding biographical and political as well as legal detail, Zelden reminds us of the courage and coolness of the men who refused to lie down under the weight of legally sponsored oppression. He notes how, at the local and national levels, lawyers for the National Association for the Advancement of Colored People engaged in their own tussle for control of the litigation. He lays out the arguments of both sides with admirable clarity and limns in the consequences of failure for both sides. This was a long and drawn-out fight, and he stays its course. Most important, he puts the case in the context of evolving constitutional and political ideas of the first half of the twentieth century, fast becoming the forgotten era of American history.

The result of the Court's decision in *Smith v. Allwright* not only affected the black people of Texas. It redrew the boundary between public and private action in constitutional law and, thus, laid the groundwork for many civil rights cases to come. It also redefined the Court's involvement in what had been a hands-off area of "political questions" and led to the Court's participation in voter reapportionment cases. If the case is not as famous now as *Brown v. Board of Education* or *Baker v. Carr,* perhaps this study will help elevate it to the first-rank position that it deserves.

{ *The Battle for the Black Ballot* }

# ACKNOWLEDGMENTS

The truism that no book is written alone is very true in this instance. Many individuals and organizations have aided me in the completion of this book. And I am grateful for all of their help and support.

Most of the archival research for this book was completed during a week-long research trip in spring 2002. I am grateful for the financial support of the Farquhar College of Arts and Science's Faculty Development Fund, which helped defray the costs of that trip.

I am also grateful for the gracious help that I received from a number of research librarians and archivists. In particular, Barbara Rust at the National Archives, Fort Worth Branch, and Michael Widner of the University of Texas Law Library were invaluable to the success of this project.

My colleagues in the Division of Humanities at Nova Southeastern University provided not only moral support but also ready ears, welcoming shoulders, and critical perceptiveness as I coped with the stresses associated with writing a book. I am especially thankful to the director of the Division of Humanities, Ben Mulvey, the department staff (Santa Alemonte, Catherine Araujo, Veronica Briones, and Zulma Martinez), and Professors Stephen Levitt, Gary Gershman, Jim Doan, and Tim Dixon. Tim Dixon also read each of the chapters, and his comments proved most helpful.

Longtime friends Lee Walzer, Brad Cohen, David and Heidi Needleman, Robin Sherman, Ric Burns, Connie Killebrew, David Narrett, Connie Anderson, and Judy Harris all provided much-needed support and encouragement. So too did my in-laws, Norm and Janet Rodseth, Judy Rodseth, and Pat Scobie. Carol Crespo's advice and support also proved essential to my mental health and, hence, to the completion of the project.

I would also like to thank the instructors and students of the South Florida Academy of Martial Arts. That the acquisition of a second obsession made the writing of this book easier may seem counter-intuitive, but it is true nonetheless.

Not enough can be said about Peter Hoffer, Mike Briggs, and the entire staff at the University Press of Kansas. Their support in the writing, and especially the revising, of this book was beyond estimate.

I am especially grateful to Peter for his insightful advice regarding the original draft of the manuscript and to Joseph Brown for his careful copyediting.

R. B. Bernstein — colleague, friend, and partner in crime — not only provided essential moral and technical support but also read and commented on every word that I wrote. The result is a much better book.

This book would not have the form that it has today without the training that I received from my graduate adviser, Harold M. Hyman. While the learning process was often frustrating and even painful, whatever skills I possess as a historian originate in his teachings. From my first day as a graduate student — when he told me to pick a topic and start researching and writing about it — to advice given over the last decade and a half, Professor Hyman has provided me with a model of dedication and ability that I have sought to emulate.

I would also like to thank my family — my mother, Janice; my sister, Renee; my wife, Lynn; and my daughter, Miriam — with as strong a thanks as possible. More than anyone else, they had to put up with the obsessiveness that is my normal writing mode. I know that it was often not easy to be around me, and I am indebted to their forebearance and support.

Finally, I would like to dedicate this book to my mother, Janice R. Zelden, without whom it would never have been written. Some twenty years ago, when I was struggling with the decision whether to attend graduate school (which is what I wanted to do) or law school (which is what my father very strongly wanted me to do), my mother said the magic words, "Why don't you go ahead and give history a try?" The rest, as they say, is history — or, more accurately, a career in history. I haven't looked back since.

# INTRODUCTION

His name was Dr. Lonnie Smith, and he wanted to vote in the Texas Democratic Party primary. It seemed like such a simple request. A lifelong resident of Houston, Smith knew the issues of the day, caring deeply about them. As a dentist, he was well educated and capable of making reasoned choices as a voter. As a believer in the tenets of the Democratic Party (in every general election up to this time in which he had voted, Smith had voted Democratic), he was ready and willing to play his part in shaping the party's future by means of his vote. And, anyhow, as a registered voter able to vote in the general election, Smith saw no logical reason why he should not be able to do the same in the primary. Yet he was barred from voting in the Democratic primary. For the year was 1940, and Smith was African American. This simple fact changed everything.

Since 1903, Texas blacks had been barred from voting in the Democratic primary by popular consensus, Democratic Party rules, and (from 1923 to 1927) state statutes. The Democratic Party was an organization for whites only. By 1940, the controlling principle read in part: "Only white citizens of the State of Texas . . . shall be eligible for membership in the Democratic Party and entitled to participate in its deliberations." Whatever his many other qualifications as a voter, Smith was, as an African American, legally barred from joining the Democratic Party and, as a nonmember, legally forbidden from voting in the party's primary elections. These were the rules. If Smith wanted to vote, he could wait for the general election in November. End of story. Or not, as events ultimately turned out.

For Smith was an officer in the Houston branch of the National Association for the Advancement of Colored People (NAACP), and, by 1940, the NAACP had been fighting against white-only primaries (hereafter the *all-white primary*, or *AWP*) for almost twenty years. Part of a much wider attack on race-based segregation and discrimination, the NAACP's assault on the AWP had to this date proved a long, frustrating, and, ultimately, fruitless endeavor. Despite repeated forays in the federal courts and even some apparent victories in the Supreme Court, the AWP remained both the law and the brutal reality in Texas blacks' lives — in fact, in the lives of African Americans across the

South. Yet the goal, both within the NAACP and for Texas's black community generally, remained strong: to end the ban on black voting in the Texas Democratic Party primary elections.

The reason for this ongoing commitment to change (as will be described in more detail in the chapters that follow) lay in the South's unique political dynamic: in the South, only one political party mattered, and that was the Democratic Party. As of 1940, no Texas Republican had been elected to a major state or federal office in over seventy years. In some parts of the state, the Republicans' drought extended back even further. In fact, in many local elections, the Republicans did not even run a candidate. Similar intervals and results could be found across the South.

Given that the Democratic nominee always won the election in the South — at least after the demise of Populism in the 1890s — the AWP made voting in the general election (or a Republican primary where one was held) a largely meaningless act. It also made the Democratic primary the prime forum for making one's electoral choices known. It was here, and only here, that the state's political leaders were chosen. Barred by both party rules and, for a time, state law from this primary, Texas blacks were unable to help select the Democratic Party candidates for office — even where they had somehow managed to register to vote — and, thus, to have a say in the running of state government.

Legal bans on African American participation in Democratic primaries therefore meant the effective and complete disfranchisement of the black community. The AWP was segregation's safety net. Where other forms of race-based vote denial — poll taxes, literacy and "understanding" clauses, racial gerrymandering — failed to keep out all black voters, the AWP kept the few who slipped through from the one election that had real political impact. It was with this in mind that every Southern state adopted some form of the AWP between 1896 and 1915.

Texas, however, depended on the AWP to a much greater extent than did other Southern states. For reasons that will be explained in chapter 2, Texas Democrats placed most of their vote denial faith in the combination of poll taxes and the AWP. The literacy tests and understanding clauses adopted by other Southern states never gained a foothold in Texas. This fact magnified the importance of the AWP there. More than just a safety net, the AWP was in Texas the gate barring African American political participation itself.

*Smith v. Allwright* — as Dr. Smith's case against the Democratic AWP would come to be known — would change all this. Organized and led by the NAACP's Legal Defense and Education Fund (LDF), and argued by the LDF's lead counsel, Thurgood Marshall, the case quickly became much, much more than one man's drive to have a meaningful say in the political process. Fought out over a two-year period in courtrooms ranging from the Houston-based Southern District of Texas to the Fifth Circuit Court of Appeals in New Orleans and, ultimately, the Supreme Court, *Smith* was one of the first truly significant — and effective — victories by Thurgood Marshall and the LDF against Jim Crow segregation. True, at the time it remained unclear whether the Supreme Court's 1944 ruling that the Texas Democratic Party was an "agency of the state," and, hence, prohibited by the Fourteenth and Fifteenth Amendments to the Constitution from denying any citizen the right to vote on the basis of race alone, would have any real impact. (It would, in fact, take a series of cases, described in chapter 6, to finally kill off the remnants of the AWP.) However, before long, the message that the AWP was dead had become very clear as blacks in Texas and across the South joined the Democratic Party and voted in significant numbers for the first time in over half a century. The AWP was dead, and *Smith* was the blade that delivered the killing stroke. (Of course, the fight for a truly *effective* African American vote would take an additional twenty-five to fifty years, but this does not lessen the importance of *Smith* as the first major victory in this fight.)

*Smith*'s importance goes beyond simply voting, however. The victory in *Smith* was the first in a series of legal victories in the late 1940s and early 1950s — including 1946's *Morgan v. Virginia* (desegregation in interstate bus travel), 1948's *Shelley v. Kraemer* (barring restrictive covenants for housing), and 1950's *Sweatt v. Painter* (requiring that separate graduate education facilities had to be equal in *fact*, not just in name) — all of which laid the groundwork for the LDF's 1954 victory over segregated education in *Brown v. Board of Education*. *Smith* in particular provided important precedents for the *Brown* victory. For one thing, *Smith* gave the LDF hope that its litigation strategy could actually work. Up to this point, most court victories, when they occurred, had little practical impact on the fight for equal rights; by one means or another, segregationist Southern officials always seemed to find new and inventive ways to keep African Americans down. Within a few years or so of the Supreme Court's 1944 decision, however, it was clear that *Smith* was different, and this difference heartened everyone associated with the fight for civil rights. Even more important, the inclusionary and activist logic of the Supreme Court's *Smith* decision lay a foundation for the Court's expanding notions of *state action* — foundations that bore ever greater fruit in the better-known education cases that followed. In creating precedents that imposed constitutional requirements for equal treatment on outwardly private activities that were, *in reality*, infused with state influence and/or performed some form of "public function," *Smith* undermined one of the most troublesome barriers to judicial action in civil rights matters: the Fourteenth and Fifteenth Amendments' "public-action" requirements (the idea that the two amendments prohibited discrimination by government officials *only*, the more common forms of discrimination imposed by private groups or individuals being deemed beyond the scope of the Constitution's protective arm). In time, the Supreme Court would come to see most aspects of race-based discrimination as inherently connected to public power and, hence, prohibited by the Constitution. From this understanding would flow most of the important civil rights rulings of the last half-century.

In the end, *Smith v. Allwright* is an accessible case study of how matters of race, class, and power all interact to shape, not only the social, political, and economic life of the nation, but also the process by which race-based discriminations are first created and then attacked within both the legal system and the wider community. Observed closely, *Smith* points out the complex interaction between law and politics in America, notes the ongoing and convoluted evolution of racial policies within this context, underscores how national concerns and local priorities shape the litigation process, and, finally, stresses the highly contested nature of the judicial process by which we shape our public realm. For, while the initial impetus to the case may have been the wish of one man to participate in the simple act of voting, the real meanings of the attack on the Texas AWP — the drive for an open and discrimination-free ballot — aim at the heart of the entire civil rights revolution and, with it, the engine of change for much of the latter half of the twentieth century.

# CHAPTER I

# Democracy on Trial

## The Persistence of Race-Based Vote Denial in American History

For a democracy, the United States does not have a very good record on voting. For most of American history, almost as much effort has gone into denying disliked or despised groups the vote — or at least diluting the impact of their vote — as has gone into expanding the franchise. At one time or another, we have excluded individuals from voting on account of their gender, race, ethnicity, social status, place of birth, legal condition, and/or lack of wealth. Almost as varied were the methods applied to obstruct unwanted participation in the political process: literacy tests, poll taxes, violence, and other forms of intimidation were each used to limit the size of the voting population. So too were education standards, propertyholding requirements, and "moral-standing" provisions specifically designed to exclude unwanted groups from the polls. And, of course, there was the method at the heart of this book: race-restricted primary elections.

Happily, over time, conditions did improve. Despite numerous inconsistencies and delays experienced in expanding the franchise, most adult Americans today — whatever their race, gender, or economic status — have the vote. And, although problems still exist, as the 2000 presidential election controversy in Florida showed, these problems have become exceptions to the rule, not the rule itself. It may have taken a while, but the promise of American democracy has been largely met.

Still, the existence of such a long and extensive history of vote denial is deeply troubling. There are few factors more vital to the existence and continuation of representative government than the simple act of voting. To exclude voters because they are somehow not "qualified" to vote *solely* because of their gender or race or ethnic background — and judgments of inadequate qualification based on such characteristics were the normal justifications used to excuse vote denial — is undemocratic.

As the historian Alexander Keyssar notes in his history *The Right to Vote*, whereas "a nation certainly could have universal suffrage without being a democracy, a polity cannot be truly democratic without universal suffrage." Yet, well into the twentieth century, in states across the nation, numerous race- and ethnicity-based exclusions were still the norm.

Most egregious among these disenfranchisement efforts, both for its offensive nature and for its durability, was the race-based vote denial experienced by African Americans — especially those living in the South. This is neither the time nor the place to go into the long, sad history of the negative treatment by the United States of its citizens of African descent. Suffice it to say that the centuries-long effort against black voting by Southern whites was part of a much larger venture to control and oppress Southern blacks (and blacks in general nationwide). Slavery was the most monstrous of these oppressive efforts — yet the post–Civil War experience was almost as bad, the end of slavery fostering a proliferation of ever more inventive and oppressive methods of exclusion. As the political scientist Frances Fox Piven and the sociologist Richard Cloward note in *Why Americans Don't Vote*: "Disenfranchisement was part of the broader effort by the southern planter class to erect a system of political, economic, and social coercion over blacks that would permit the reestablishment of a quasi-feudal labor system [similar in scope to slavery]."

Foremost among the efforts to exclude blacks from Southern public life were rules and norms forcing them into "separate but equal" housing, transportation, schools, and eating places and other public facilities. In most cases, these separate facilities were equal in name only. To take just one example, that of segregated schools, in 1949 the annual expenditure per student in Clarendon County, South Carolina, stood at $49 for blacks and $179 for whites. Teacher/student ratios in Clarendon County varied just as widely: one teacher for every twenty-eight white students and one for every forty-seven black students. Facilities were also radically dissimilar. The whites-only school was a modern one, made of brick and stucco and equipped with indoor plumbing, a lunchroom, and a gym; the blacks-only school was made of wood and lacked indoor plumbing and eating facilities.

The existence of such a long train of race-based inequalities signifies more than a mere listing of personal suffering and race division. At its heart, segregation meant control — control at all costs, by any and all means, in order to keep power in the hands of those who already had it, Southern whites (more specifically, rich Southern whites). In their efforts to "keep blacks in their place," Southern whites were waging an all-out war of repression on their neighbors of African descent. As the historian C. Vann Woodward notes in *Origins of the New South*, in the late nineteenth century "it became standard practice to support disfranchising campaigns with white-supremacy propaganda in which race hatred, suspicion, and jealousy were whipped up to a dangerous pitch." Soon, race riots in which "white men roamed" about the city or countryside "assaulting Negroes, looting, burning, and shooting" were reported across the South. Hatred and violence, in turn, fueled the justifications of more formal types of repression, such as segregation and disenfranchisement, which in turn fueled additional hate and violence, which in turn demanded even more extreme forms of repression. And so the cycle of hate and violence justifying repression continued unchecked. By combining informal forms of violence with formal rules of segregation and exclusion, dominant Southern whites were, thus, able to impoverish and demoralize Southern blacks so much that they were easy to control and, hence, to exploit. And, whereas this control came at a high price in terms of economic stagnation, for whites as well as for blacks, it was a price that the Southern white leadership was more than willing to pay. By 1940, the white South had been successful in this effort for over two generations.

The practical result of such repressive efforts, formal and informal, was the eventual (and perhaps inevitable) expulsion of African Americans from most aspects of Southern public life. Blacks could not vote, nor could they hold public office. They were barred from riding on the same train cars as whites and, later on, exiled to the backs of public buses. The vast majority were barred by the racism of white unions and the opportunism of management from most gainful forms of employment. Prominent black leaders — in fact, any black who spoke out too loudly against the limitations imposed by segregation — faced the daily threat of death by lynching. Blacks received an inferior education, and they were forbidden to frequent the same parks, swim in the same pools, even drink from the same water fountains as whites.

All this talk of control and oppression leaves out the important question, *Why?* Why did Southern whites feel the need to oppress blacks? And why make use of vote exclusion as part of this process?

Was there something about voting that necessitated such extreme efforts to keep blacks from the polls? If so, what was this something? Moreover, why did this all occur in the South and not in the North or the West? Race hatred, and the economic, social, and political repression of African Americans, has been a national reality for most of American history, yet it was in the South that efforts to oppress blacks reached their greatest scope. Why?

The same question arises for vote denial. Voting has always been a highly contested topic in America. The list of those excluded from the franchise is much, much longer than the list of those who always could vote. In fact, with the exception of white, property-owning Protestant men, most segments of the American public (women, the poor, Indians, African Americans, Catholics, non-Christian minorities) have been denied the vote for at least a time in most, if not all, states of the Union. Yet it was in the South that vote denial reached its most blatant, intense, and extreme forms. Whites in the North and the West might have hated blacks and sought on many occasions to deny them a meaningful place in public life, but such efforts were but a part of a much wider and generally more diffuse campaign to keep power and the vote from a number of distrusted groups. Not so the South. Here, the goal was the total exclusion of a single group from *any* meaningful say in the shaping of the public realm. Why?

Why and how Southern whites fought so hard to exclude Southern blacks from the polls is a complex problem, the answers to which lie in the convergence of many historical trends. One essential factor, however, was race hatred. Racism — feelings of superiority, hatred, and distrust based on differences in skin color and other physical characteristics — has a long history in America, in the North as well as in the South. The origins and sources of this hatred form a vast, complex, and controversial line of historical inquiry. For our purposes, however, it is enough to say that, for most of this nation's history, large segments of white America distrusted, feared, and hated African Americans — in most cases merely for being different. The result was a persistent, wide-ranging national campaign of repression aimed at African Americans. From slavery, to formal and informal segregation, to the denial of basic civil rights and liberties, African Americans faced exclusions, limits, and intimidations in their daily lives. Threats of violence, not to mention actual acts of violence, were a constant reality for most

{ *The Battle for the Black Ballot* }

blacks. The unspoken message was that blacks were not wanted, and examples of this bigoted sentiment could be found nationwide.

Yet it was in the South where race hatred was most intense and racial oppression most extensive. Much of Southern society was constructed around the dictates and needs of racism. The South retained and increased its commitment to the institution of slavery following the Revolution, in the process constructing an economy, society, and culture predicated on the oppression and exploitation of blacks. The South, once again, refused to give up these economic, social, and cultural patterns even with the end of slavery. And formal, legal segregation — a multifaceted campaign to exclude blacks from nearly every aspect of public life — came into being in the South on the eve of the twentieth century.

The source of the white South's intense race hatred and extreme acts of oppression (at least in comparison to the more general hatred and oppression found nationwide) was in part a result of the region's distinct demographics. Before the late twentieth century, most African Americans lived in the South. Blacks, in fact, made up nearly half the total population of the South at the beginning, and were still a significant minority at the end, of the nineteenth century. Indeed, in some parts of the South, African Americans formed the majority. In other sections, they were merely a sizable presence within the general population. Not until the mid-twentieth century would significant numbers of African Americans migrate north and west.

This simple numerical fact magnified the effects of racism in the South. In this instance, proximity did not foster intimacy and understanding — far from it. Rather, closeness intensified the fear of the "other" that lay at the heart of racism. For, if the nightmarish visions animated by racist beliefs were actually true, if all the terrors about the dangers and wickedness of African Americans were real, then the impact of race on life in the South had to be horrific, if only because of the scope of the problem (i.e., the sheer number of African Americans found in the South). The large numbers of Southern blacks, in other words, had a multiplier effect on the fears of Southern whites. And enhanced fears inevitably seemed to lead to intensified and extreme reactions.

Numbers also help explain the importance that excluding black voting played in the workings of Southern white racism. Give Southern blacks the franchise, and they might actually elect one of their own to political office—or, worse yet, elect dozens or even hundreds of black officials. At the least, white politicians would have to concern themselves with the interests of Southern blacks, actually endorsing policies aimed at helping African Americans, if they wished to win office. To a population raised in a culture largely built on the existence of racist fears, this was an unacceptable state of affairs. Hence the need to keep blacks out of the polls at all costs.

Within the white Southern mind, exacerbating the racism engendered by the large numbers of blacks in the South and the fear of black voting were many social, political, and economic tensions within the Southern white population. The "solid South" was anything but solid. Urban against rural, rich against poor—these and other fault lines within the Southern white population were real and potentially explosive. This was especially the case in the late nineteenth century, when economic changes associated with the rise of a national market and the growth of corporate industrialism promoted both frustration and anger within the South's large, and mostly poor, rural population. Growing ever stronger as the decades passed, these feelings of frustration and anger fostered a serious political challenge to the region's established white leadership in the form of the Populist revolt at the end of the century.

A fragmented and combative white population, in turn, increased the potential threat of black voting to undermine continued white dominance of the region's governing institutions. Not that many blacks were likely to win political office, given the exclusionary tendencies of Southern life. However, where an election became very close, small numbers of isolated voters could cast decisive swing votes, effectively deciding the election's outcome. Given the tensions within the white South, the use of blacks as swing voters was a real threat, one that the established Southern white leadership took very seriously.

Whatever the causes, the widespread existence of racism among Southern whites is key to explaining the region's violent responses to efforts to achieve racial equality following the Civil War. Starting from a racist foundation, white Southerners—rich or poor—could not conceive of, let alone accept, a world based on racial equality. In their eyes, blacks were inferior and dangerous outsiders whose presence in the body politic threatened the stability of Southern society and culture. Give African Americans the vote, the argument went, and all that native-born, white Southerners held dear would be lost. Africans were, according to this view, less than fully human, as the North Carolina journalist Hinton Helper made clear in 1855 when he argued that blacks (along with other dark races), "befouled with all the social vices, with no knowledge or appreciation of free institutions or constitutional liberty," were holders of "heathenish souls and heathenish propensities." Grant such a people a voice in the governing of this nation, Helper concluded, and "be prepared to bid farewell to republicanism."

This mind-set all but mandated Southern whites' assault on equal rights for blacks. By every standard by which they defined their world (and, by the late nineteenth century, racist assumptions permeated almost every aspect of white Southern culture), allowing blacks the vote could result only in chaos and destruction. And, although (as we shall see) some Southern whites were willing to forgo their racist upbringing, most were not. In fact, it was the willingness of some poor white Southerners to abandon racism and seek to work with poor blacks in an effort to better their lives that accelerated the drive for the total exclusion of African Americans from the polls across the South.

That paradox brings us back to the white South's campaign against Southern black voting. Before the Civil War, black voting in the South was effectively a nonissue. Most Southern blacks were slaves and, as such, could not vote. And a mix of state constitutional amendments, statutory enactments, and informal intimidation kept those few Southern blacks who were not enslaved away from the polls. The Union's victory in the Civil War, however, promised a change in this state of affairs — or at least this was the hope of those advocating political rights for the newly freed Southern black population. The Thirteenth Amendment's requirement that "neither slavery nor involuntary servitude . . . shall exist within the United States" seemed, to the amendment's Republican authors and most Northerners and Westerners, to mean that newly freed blacks would acquire all aspects of freedom, including citizenship and the right to vote. Whatever their personal views on the issue of race and rights, all agreed that newly freed Southern blacks needed the basic tools of freedom — among them the rights to make contracts, to travel, and to participate in the political process — if their freedom were to be real and lasting.

Unfortunately, no one explained this to the South's white inhabitants, nor would they have listened. Regaining power soon after the war's end under presidential Reconstruction, officials and legislatures of the former Confederate states adopted harsh laws, known as Black Codes, aimed at depriving the newly freed slaves of all the substance · of freedom. This included the vote.

The Union's response was the Fourteenth Amendment. Aimed squarely at the Black Codes, the Fourteenth Amendment defined national citizenship, upheld a citizen's right to due process under the law, and prohibited public discriminations that undermined the "privileges or immunities of citizens of the United States." One of those privileges and immunities was the right to vote. Congressional Republicans hoped that merging the votes of black freedmen with white Southern Unionists would soon give Southern blacks the means to protect themselves from discrimination by electing candidates of their choice to public office. Yet, for this result to become a reality, blacks had to be assured an effective franchise. This proved a difficult task. For, whereas *in theory* the Fourteenth Amendment meant that the states could not exclude a particular group from the franchise without a very good reason, *in practice* the definition of how good that reason had to be was open to interpretation. White Southerners took full advantage of this loophole, refusing to abide by the law, and attacking blacks' right to vote with public discrimination wherever possible and with private intimidation in all cases.

Frustrated by the lack of black electoral success and the taunting appearance of Southern white defiance, Congress responded with a third constitutional amendment, one aimed explicitly at the right to vote. This time Congress was serious. Black males had the right to vote, the Fifteenth Amendment declared, and no state had the right to deny them that vote: "The right of citizens of the United States to vote shall not be denied or abridged by the United States or by any State on account of race, color, or previous condition of servitude." Combined with the equal protection clause of the Fourteenth Amendment, the Constitution's intent could not be made much clearer, or so congressional Republicans believed.

And, for a time, things actually seemed to change. In 1867 and 1868, blacks across the South joined with white Southern Republicans to elect large numbers of delegates, many of them black, to new

{ *The Battle for the Black Ballot* }

state constitutional conventions. These Republican-dominated conventions, in turn, produced extremely liberal constitutions granting full civil rights, including the right to vote, to black Southerners. Hundreds of thousands of blacks quickly registered to vote, and, in later elections, they exercised this right — often for black candidates. Ultimately, more than six hundred blacks would be elected to offices in the state governments organized under the Reconstruction state constitutions, including one black governor (in Louisiana), six lieutenant governors, hundreds of legislators, and numerous state treasurers, secretaries of state, and superintendents of education. Many more blacks held local and county offices, including such positions as county supervisor, mayor, sheriff, judge, and justice of the peace.

By the early 1870s, however, things began to fall apart. Most white Southerners disliked the entire concept of Reconstruction and opposed the Republican- and black-led governments organized under this process. As early as 1866, white terrorist organizations — the Ku Klux Klan being the best known — mobilized to oppose all efforts to transform the South's social relations. With the rise of Republican-led government, these groups began a wave of race-based violence and terror that spread across the South. Republican Party meetings were broken up. Prominent blacks were attacked and often killed. Before long, even average blacks were assaulted for being "impudent" toward whites or not knowing their place; in 1870 alone, the death toll was in the hundreds and the number injured even greater. In the worst incidents, white mobs attacked entire groups of blacks, terrorizing most, and killing many. In one 1873 incident alone, in Colfax, Louisiana, a white mob attacked and trapped 150 blacks in the county courthouse for three days; before the riot ended, over fifty blacks had been massacred — many after they had tried surrendering under a white flag.

Adding to black Americans' electoral woes were changes in the national commitment to Reconstruction and an expansive black franchise. By 1873, faced with the need to cut the federal budget during an economic depression, and concerned about the fading support for Reconstruction shown by a Northern population turning increasingly inward in its interests, the Grant administration put the brakes on vigorous prosecution of Southern race-based discrimination. In that same year, the Supreme Court handed down its decision in the *Slaughterhouse Cases.* Although not explicitly concerned with issues of race (the case had to do with state regulation of slaughterhouses in New Orleans), the case had profound consequences for civil rights — and for voting. In his opinion for the Court, Justice Samuel F. Miller ruled that the Fourteenth Amendment should be limited to its original purpose of guaranteeing the privileges and immunities of former black slaves. Unfortunately, in doing this, Miller identified some privileges and immunities as national and some as local and, thus, severed national citizenship from state citizenship. Worse yet, in defining exactly which privileges and immunities were national and which local, Miller placed the civil rights most important to everyday life, including those protecting voting rights, in the *state* category. The result (as the historians Harold Hyman and William Wiecek note in their *Equal Justice under Law*) "consigned [blacks] to the ingenuities, subterfuges, and legal chicane of white Democrats already returning to power in the South" by means of the sort of intimidations and frauds that the two enforcement acts were supposed to halt. Three years later, in *United States v. Cruikshank* (1876), the Supreme Court unanimously struck down the Civil Rights Act of 1871, holding that murder — even the mass murder of over one hundred blacks in a race riot — did not deprive the injured of their federally protected civil rights. Murder, the Court declared, was a state matter best handled in the state courts. *United States v. Reese*, another 1876 decision, produced a similar restrictive result. A final blow came with the so-called Compromise of 1877 and the end of formal Reconstruction. No longer would the national government concern itself with the South's handling of race relations; combined with the Supreme Court's limiting of the civil rights amendments in *Slaughterhouse*, *Cruikshank*, and *Reese*, this agreement effectively abandoned blacks to the not-so-gentle mercies of Southern whites.

As for black voting rights, the end of Reconstruction and the subsequent abandonment of Southern blacks spurred a sharp reversal of course by the Southern states' political systems toward vote denial. Southern whites still could not accept the idea of black equality. In their eyes, blacks were not capable of being equal to whites. In fact (to quote a petition to Congress of a group of Alabama whites in 1868), because blacks were "wholly unacquainted with the principles of free Governments, improvident, disinclined to work, credulous yet suspicious, dishonest, untruthful, incapable of self-restraint, and easily impelled . . . into folly and crime," they were totally unfit to hold the franchise. "How can it be otherwise," these concerned Southern whites asked, "than that they [blacks] will bring, to the great injury of themselves as well as of us and our children, blight, crime, ruin and barbarism on this fair land?" With such visions in their heads, how could white Southerners *not* fight against the black vote? Many whites decided that they had no choice.

Once freed by the end of Reconstruction to act as they wished, Southern state governments, dominated by whites, quickly adopted a series of practices and procedures explicitly aimed at denying blacks the vote. Combining unofficial intimidation and violence with official impediments to black voting, the result was the slow, but steady, disenfranchisement of Southern black males by the turn of the century (black women were already barred from voting on account of their gender).

Whites began their attack on black suffrage in the 1870s and 1880s by first seeking to dilute the impact of black voting. Some states passed laws granting the legislature or the governor the power to appoint local government officials who had previously been selected by popular vote. Many Southern state legislatures also gerrymandered voting districts to minimize the impact of large black voting populations. Alabama, for instance, divided its black majorities into multiple voting districts so that blacks, no longer a majority in any one district, could always be outvoted by unified white voters. Mississippi took the opposite approach, gathering its blacks into a single district so that their votes could swing only a single election out of the five or six districts contested. In either case, the result was the same: even where Southern blacks voted in large numbers, they could not determine an election's outcome so long as white majorities voted as a group. Whites achieved a similar result at the county level by adopting at-large voting systems to replace the more traditional single-member districts. Denied the power that localized numbers could bring, blacks were once again effectively cut out of the electoral process.

Building on vote dilution schemes, white Southern officials also adopted rules and procedures making it increasingly difficult for blacks to exercise their voting rights. For example, hoping to discourage blacks from voting, election officials in Georgia, Mississippi, and Louisiana set up polling places in areas inconvenient for blacks. Many were placed at distant locations or in the middle of white sections of the town or county; some were put in businesses owned by known opponents of African American voting. Such situations were intimidating at least, and often outright dangerous, for blacks brave enough to attempt to vote. A parallel approach was to limit the hours when predominantly black polling places were open; a few local officials refused to open these polling places at all. A third popular trick played on black illiteracy. In 1882, South Carolina adopted what it called the Eight-Box Ballot Law. Under this rule, ballots for individual offices had to be placed in separate ballot boxes. Put your ballot in the wrong box, and it would not be counted. And, although the boxes were usually labeled properly, this meant little to illiterate black voters unable to read the labels. As if this were not enough, many election supervisors shifted the boxes around periodically. Countless misplaced — and, hence, uncounted — ballots were the result.

More effective were laws designed either to keep blacks from being listed on the voting rolls or to allow local officials to purge them from the lists. The most prevalent approach was illustrated by an 1873 Georgia law that permitted local election supervisors to close their registration rolls to new applicants *except* during those periods when black farmers were too busy to register, such as planting or harvest time. North Carolina and Alabama had similar laws. Some states added the requirement that voters show proof of registration before they could vote or face immediate disqualification. Given the long gap between registering and voting in most Southern states, this was a request that many blacks (as well as whites) could not meet. Virginia went one step further, mandating separate registration books for white and black voters; not surprisingly, black registration books regularly came up missing when blacks wished to register or were lost on voting day. And then there was the increasingly common practice in all the Southern states of adding those crimes considered most likely to be committed by blacks — arson, bigamy, and petty theft — to the list of felonies that disqualified one from voting ever again. White crimes, on the other hand, such as grand larceny, invoked no such limits.

The most popular means of excluding blacks from the franchise was the poll tax. Many states already had such laws on their books, remnants of the old colonial property-based voting rules. As a result, all they had to do to exclude unwanted voters was make payment of such taxes mandatory and then increase the amount of tax required to vote; raise the total enough, and most blacks would be barred from the vote. This was what Georgia achieved in 1877 when it not only increased the amount of tax owed to vote but made payment of the tax cumulative before voters could cast their ballots. As a result, in order to vote blacks had to pay, not just the present year's tax, but all the accumulated back taxes imposed by state law. Miss one year, and the cumulative and indefinite nature of the poll tax made it nearly impossible for poor blacks ever to vote again.

The poll tax was brutally efficient in keeping poor blacks from the polls; indeed, in 1908, Alfred Stone described the poll tax as "the most effective bar to Negro suffrage ever devised." By the early twentieth century, every Southern state used some sort of poll tax to deny blacks the vote. And, although one unanticipated consequence of the poll tax was to disenfranchise many poor whites, this was a cost that Southern white leaders were willing to shoulder to keep blacks from the voting booth.

Of course, poll taxes did little to hinder blacks who had the resources to pay. As late as the 1890s, many blacks remained on the voting lists. In Louisiana, the number stood at 130,000; Alabama had 181,000 black voters; and other states showed similar numbers. More ingenuity was needed to realize conservative whites' dreams of excluding blacks from the vote. By the early 1890s, in the midst of the Populist-inspired agrarian revolt, Southern white elites felt motivated to do more, expanding their attacks on black voting to the next stage: total vote denial based on race. As one delegate to Virginia's 1901 constitutional convention noted, the intent after 1890 was "to disfranchise every Negro that [they] could disfranchise under the Constitution of the United States, and as few white people as possible." And disenfranchise they did.

Although still operating through the medium of technically race-neutral structures, between 1890 and 1905 governments across the South updated their election laws and revised their constitutions to exclude black voting more fully. The first and most successful of these disenfranchisement plans arose in Mississippi. Written into a new state constitution in 1890, the four-step "Mississippi Plan" included a $2 poll tax payable before registration; a literacy test in which voters had to read, understand, or interpret any section of the state constitution to the satisfaction of a white (and usually hostile) election official; long-term residency rules demanding two years' domicile within the state and one year's within the voting district; and permanent disenfranchisement for crimes felt most likely to be committed by blacks.

Extremely popular with local whites, the Mississippi Plan also appealed to whites in the other Southern states, each of which soon copied Mississippi's new approach to vote denial. In 1895, South Carolina required all voters to read and/or explain any section of the state constitution provided by the local voting registrar and also to meet a two-year residency requirement. Louisiana added similar literacy requirements to its constitution in 1898, along with a new poll tax and rules denying felons the vote unless pardoned by the governor. Concerned with the potential of these rules to expel poor and illiterate whites from the polls, the state also adopted a grandfather clause that allowed those who had voted before 1867 (when blacks could not vote) or whose fathers and grandfathers had voted then to waive the new requirements. Two years later, North Carolina imposed a poll tax and adopted literacy tests administered by local registrars (who had full discretion as to which parts of the state constitution applicants had to read) as its primary tool of vote denial; the state added a grandfather clause similar to Louisiana's to protect poor white voters. Similar outcomes followed, as Alabama in 1901, Virginia in 1902, Texas in 1904, and Georgia in 1908 revised their constitutions.

The results of such efforts were immediate and drastic. By 1900, all forms of voter participation in Mississippi had declined to a mere 17 percent; black turnout stood at less than 9,000 out of a potential 147,000 voting-age blacks (essentially those who had voted before 1890). In Louisiana, registered black voters declined by 99 percent to just 1,300 in 1904. Alabama had only 3,000 registered black voters in 1902. In Georgia, only 4 percent of black males were even registered to vote as of 1910. Texas saw black voting decline to a mere 5,000 votes in 1906. In fact, across the entire region, voter turnout fell from a high of 85 percent of all voters during Reconstruction to less than 50 percent for whites, and single-digit percentages for blacks, in the new century.

By the early 1900s, the fight against black voting was largely complete. Most Southern states had revised their constitutions and statutes to exclude blacks (and many poor whites) from the vote by using techniques similar to Mississippi's. As of 1915, no Southern state was without some sort of vote denial program. Yet one final step remained. Even with poll taxes and literacy requirements, felony exclusions and grandfather clauses, some blacks still managed to gain the franchise. If black disenfranchisement were to be made total, if the very meaning of the vote and its usefulness for blacks were to be negated, then the right to vote in the general election had to be separated from the right to vote in the party primaries — and in particular in the all-important Democratic Party primary. The last step was what came to be called the *all-white primary*. What follows is the story of that primary and its eventual demise by court action.

# CHAPTER 2

# To Exclude and Oppress
## The Evolution of
## the Texas All-White Primary

On the surface, the South's decision to turn to the all-white primary (AWP) as a means of race-based vote denial seems an odd choice. Southern whites had so many other less explicit, yet equally effective, ways of excluding blacks from the franchise. In fact, most Southern states made extensive use of technically race-neutral vote denial techniques. Literacy and "understanding" tests, complex registration rules, felony exclusions, and especially poll taxes — each had a home in the South's extensive armory of race-based disenfranchisement.

The AWP was different. AWPs were race specific. By definition, only those able to pass other race-neutral vote denial tests could vote in the Democratic Party primary. This meant that any African American voters denied access to Southern Democratic primaries were excluded *solely* because they were black. Had there been any other reason to exclude them, they would not have been in a position to vote in the Democratic Party's primaries in the first place. Race, and race alone, was the sole determinant.

Of course, *in practice*, the supposedly race-neutral types of vote exclusion were intensely race conscious in both their application and their impact. Picking only those crimes most likely to be committed by African Americans or granting extensive discretion to racist local election officials in enforcing literacy or understanding rules was an invitation to race-specific discrimination — an invitation willingly accepted across the South. In fact, it was because poll taxes did *not* discriminate between white and black voters that many Southern states imposed grandfather clauses allowing poor whites — but not poor blacks — an exception allowing them to vote.

Still, if one looked only to the letter of the law, such exclusionary techniques ran afoul of neither the Fourteenth Amendment's equal protection provisions nor the Fifteenth Amendment's ban on race-based vote denial. By contrast, the AWP did. Yet, by the end of the 1910s, almost every Southern state had imposed some form of the AWP. Why? And, more important for our purposes, why would Texas alone among Southern states choose the AWP as the foundation for its disenfranchisement efforts, especially when other forms of race-based vote denial were equally as effective (and, in some cases, even more so)?

The answers to these questions—both the general and the specific—lie in the unique mix of race hatred that lay at the core of Southern social relations, the politics of class as practiced at the end of the nineteenth century, and the negative context of this nation's built-in, historic tendency toward vote denial. When viewed through the lens of these three historical trends, the South's decision to squeeze out every last exclusion, even at the risk of running afoul of the civil rights amendments' provisions, makes sense—a sad and brutal sense, but sense nonetheless. Paranoid on social and cultural levels, torn by internal class dissensions and political infighting, and fearful of Northern interference—not to mention being conditioned to view voting as an act best left only to those deserving of the right—Southern whites felt that they had little choice but to act as they did. And, given the Supreme Court's clear unwillingness to apply the civil rights amendments aggressively to protect African Americans, the risks of adopting a race-specific method of disenfranchisement seemed small.

The same holds true for Texas's decision to base its disenfranchisement efforts on the poll tax and the AWP. Like the rest of the South, white Texans objected to race equality as a rule and faced serious internal disputes within their own ranks. What differed in Texas was the context of the conflict within the white community and the racial implications of white Texas's distrust of the state's black population—not to mention the presence of a second minority group, Mexican Americans, to complicate matters. In the context of Texas's unique historical and political environment, emphasizing protection of white political power at the primary level made sense. Texas Democratic politics could be among the most contentious in the South. The combination of Populism's electoral fallout (which in Texas was especially complex) and the need to exclude blacks without filtering out too many easily controlled and managed Mexican American voters in South Texas dictated the state's reliance on poll taxes and the AWP. So too did rifts within the Democratic Party's established leadership, as some Texas politicians reached out a partial hand of help to the former Populists and others did not. In the end, the application of an extensive and disenfranchising poll tax combined with Populism's political fallout mandated the need for an AWP if white Texans were to maintain political harmony and hegemony.

Still, the justifications and motivations found in the Texas context resonated to different degrees across the South. Texas might have been extreme as to the white majority's need for controlled disenfranchisement and, hence, unique in the choice of its disenfranchisement methods, but each of these features of the Texas electoral regime fell within the white Southern norm. In this way, the Texas case provides an enlightening perspective on the rise, evolution, and eventual decline of the AWP in general.

As the twentieth century dawned, Texas was in its fourth decade of social, economic, and political turmoil. As it had across the South in general, the end of the Civil War had sparked an extended period of strife and discord within Texas. The imposition of Reconstruction, the rise of a black-friendly Republican government in response to Reconstruction, and the eventual (and bloody) revolt against both presaged the conflicts to follow. At their core, the tensions and conflicts that Texans experienced during these forty years were the product of socioeconomic transformations affecting the nation — transformations magnified and distorted by the state's unique racial and class tensions. Immigration, urbanization, industrialization, mechanization, and the growing disparity of wealth and power between farm and city all brought new ideas and lifestyles to the American people. While for some these changes were shifts to a desired future, for others they were devastating losses destroying a beloved way of life. This was especially the case in Texas.

In 1870, Texas was still a frontier state. Since, statewide, there was less than 1,000 miles of railroad track (although this figure had increased to 1,578 miles by 1873), most Texans lived isolated lives, scratching out a living as subsistence farmers miles away from local markets — let alone national ones. Travel was by horseback, stagecoach, and oxcart, making it difficult, if not impossible, for farmers to ship their products to market. Most farmers of necessity grew grains and vegetables for their own nourishment while making their own clothes and tools and building their own shelters with only those materials close at hand. What cities and towns existed were small and closely tied to the local farming communities that surrounded them through a network of barter relationships.

By 1900, all this had changed. Connected by extensive and still expanding railroad networks (by 1904, Texas had over ten thousand miles of track crisscrossing the state), Texans had become part of a growing national and even international urban-industrial market economy, serving that economy as an important supplier of raw materials. Across the state, a number of mostly extractive business enterprises grew in response to the increased access to markets provided by the railroads. Cattle ranching, lumber, and, later, oil drilling benefited from this connection, as did local small manufacturing concerns encompassing leather goods, farm implements, and cotton textile production. Banking and other urban-based services grew hand in hand with this increase, expanding to meet the growing demands of local industry and commerce. The most affected sector of the economy, however, was agriculture.

With adequate transportation now available via the railroads, commercially based farming — in particular the growing of cotton for sale on the open market — soon replaced subsistence agriculture as the norm across the state. Farmers turned to commercial agriculture for a number of reasons. For one thing, access to the railroads meant that they could undertake commercial farming. For many Texas farmers, subsistence farming had been a necessity, not a preference. Farming for the market meant money, and money meant the ability to buy the manufactured goods that made life more comfortable. For another, commercial agriculture also made it possible for farmers to pay off their taxes, which, after 1865, were due in cash. In the end, however, most farmers turned to commercial agriculture because they had little choice.

Texas's population grew rapidly following the Civil War. In 1860, Texas had 604,215 residents; forty years later, this number stood at 3,048,710. Most of this growth came as a result of an influx of white Southerners seeking a new start following the war — many of whom arrived cash poor. To survive, new immigrant farmers had either to take out loans to pay for the seed and tools they needed to work their newly acquired farms (and interest rates on these "crop-lien" loans from local merchants could run as high as 60 percent) or to become tenant farmers, sharecropping someone else's land. Sharecropping was a system in which a tenant farmer provided the labor to grow a crop on land provided by someone else (using seed and tools provided by that same landowner or a local merchant) in return for a share of the profits from the resulting crop. Often this "share" proved small (or even nonexistent) as landowners took 50 percent or more of the resulting yield as rent and local merchants took an additional percentage of the crop in return for seed, tools, and other supplies purchased during the year. In either case, payment of these loans demanded the shift to commercial agriculture. If bankers or merchants were going to lend money to farmers — and agriculture was an inherently risky endeavor — they were going to make sure that the loan could be paid back in hard currency. No cash, no loans. The need for hard cash to pay off debts thus *forced* tenant farmers (and poor farmers in general) to grow those crops that would sell best on the open market — and, for most, that crop was cotton.

Of all the crops that Texas farmers could plant, cotton was the most productive. As the economic historian Gavin Wright notes in his *Old South, New South:* "Cotton was far more valuable *per acre* than were alternative uses of land." Cotton withstood drought better than alternative crops; it exhausted the soil of nutrients less than alternative crops; and, most important, it brought the highest return on investment compared to any alternative crop. This last advantage carried the most weight with Texas farmers. If cotton brought the greatest monetary return, then cotton was what these farmers planted; without access to land and/or loans from rich planters and merchants, farmers would not have been able to plant *any* crop at all, and that was not an option.

High levels of cotton production came at a heavy price, however: the rapid growth of tenant farming. Over time, declining cotton prices (which fell from a high of 16.5 cents per pound in 1869 to a low of 5.7 cents in 1898) so undermined the value of harvests that crop yields failed to cover farmers' debts. As one East Texas farmer noted in 1878: "Money is hardly to be had, at all, outside of the Banks. And there the interest is ruinous. I know of nobody making money in our Country." As the century progressed, an increasing number of small landowning farmers found themselves losing their farms to foreclosure and becoming tenants on farms they once owned. Combined with the large number of farmers who started out as tenants and sharecroppers (and who were required by landowners to plant cotton), the result was a never-ending cycle in which cotton farming led to increasing debt, which then led to a growth in tenant farming, which inevitably led to more debt and tenant farming. So the cycle continued, until, by 1900, fully 49.7 percent of all Texas farmers were debt-ridden tenants on the land they farmed.

The political consequences of this economic and social shift were explosive. Trapped in a declining cycle of debt and poverty, half the state's white farmers — and an even greater percentage of the state's African American farmers — were living under conditions of near peonage (debt slavery). Tenant farmers were now part of a national market economy the dictates of which they neither controlled nor fully understood; the only answer they had to their dilemmas was to grow more cotton and hope. Cotton prices kept falling, yet farmers *had* to grow cotton if they were going to get the cash they needed to pay off even a portion of their debts. What other options did they have? Unlike the debt-ridden farmers of the past, giving up and moving to new lands and opportunities was not an option. Where would they go? By the 1890s, the public lands were almost completely gone. Southern cities, in turn, lacked industrial jobs that they could take. And most tenant farmers lacked the cash resources to move elsewhere. So, despite growing as much cotton as they could, with every passing year tenant farmers found their debts — and their problems — growing.

The vast majority of Texas farmers were trapped by events beyond their control and growing more trapped with every passing year. Their response, not surprisingly, was one of increasing anger. Farmers could understand and accept the devastation of drought or the loss of their crops to flood; these were typical elements of any farmer's life, acts of God beyond their control. What they could not understand or accept was the steady, inexorable decline in their standards of living. It seemed that, the harder they worked, the more they fell behind. Something — or, more accurately, someone — had to be at fault. The questions were, Who is at fault? and, more important, How can we stop them?

Beginning in the late 1870s, Texas farmers began to find answers to both these questions. Put forth by a succession of reform and political protest movements, these explanations and proposed remedies gave the farmers a range of possible responses to their horrific situation.

Some involved working within the established political system while focusing on self-help remedies; others stressed political reform and promoted the creation of third parties. All expressed the farm community's frustration and anger. In the end, divisions and conflicts within the rural electorate — combined with the concerted efforts of the politically dominant Democrats to retain the support of farmers — would undermine these reform efforts. Still, for almost thirty years, a class-based, rural-centered political revolt shook the foundations of Texas politics.

It all began in the mid-1870s with the Granger Movement, which blamed farmers' financial losses on the railroads' (and other similar interstate corporations') dishonest and fraudulent practices — all of which, Grangers contended, cheated and exploited the farm community. Numbering some forty-five thousand members at its peak, the Texas branch of the Grange (which originated and was strongest in the Midwest) called for Texas farmers to create their own agricultural cooperatives to compete with interstate corporations. In this way, the argument went, farmers could assure fair and honest business practices and, thus, overcome the economic woes that troubled them. The Grangers left political reform to the Democrats.

The Greenback Party offered a more radical explanation of the farmers' woes. A full-fledged third-party movement, the Greenback Party originated in the South and Midwest in response to the same negative forces that produced the Grange. The Greenbackers, however, explained these problems at a much higher level of abstraction than did the Grangers. Whereas the Grange blamed the railroads for the farmers' difficulties, the Greenback Party blamed the national government's fiscal policy of hard currency (coins only) and high tariffs. These policies, party leaders argued, hurt farmers by depressing prices for farm products, raising prices of the manufactured products that they needed to purchase, and generally making it hard for farmers and others to pay off their debts. Their answer was to print more paper money (greenbacks) as a spur to inflation. Inflation, so the argument went, would raise the price of agricultural commodities by about one-third. More important, it would allow debtors to pay off their loans with inflated money (which, thus, would be easier to earn). Freed from debt by inflated currency, the argument ran, farmers could then afford to diversify their crops, lessening their reliance on market forces to survive, and breaking the endless cycle of debt and despair.

Organized in the late 1870s, the Texas State Greenback Party held its first convention in Waco in 1878. The initial results proved promising. While its gubernatorial candidate, William H. Hamman, lost the election, the party did win ten seats in the state legislature and elected George W. "Wash" Jones of Bastrop to Congress. Unfortunately, subsequent elections saw these electoral gains dwindle in numbers and effect, as internal disputes over whether to ally with the Republicans in a fusion ticket or to maintain ties to the dominant Democrats split the Greenbackers' leadership. Still, the Greenback Party's explanation of rural poverty was enticing, and the party retained strong support among the more radical elements of Texas's rural communities throughout the 1880s. By this time, however, a new rural reform movement was taking root: the Farmers' Alliance.

Originating in the depressed north central Texas region known as the Cross Timbers, the Farmers' Alliance shared the Grange's and the Greenbackers' understanding of the source of the farmers' plight and adopted most of their proposed remedies as well. However, unlike the Grange, the Alliance was much more willing to use politics to force reform, and, unlike the Greenback Party, it supported a wider range of remedies and solutions than simple inflation. Still, at its core, the Alliance agreed with the earlier movements that the farmers' plight was caused by "shameful abuses" caused by "arrogant capitalists and powerful corporations." Its solution to this problem lay in a mix of government regulations and collective self-help reforms. Support for labor unions and farmers' cooperatives, the abolition of convict leasing, an updated and more open banking system, and taxation on corporate assets pegged at their fair market value were some of the Alliance's proposed reforms. So too were the free coinage of silver and gold to induce inflation and the creation of a national commission to regulate interstate commerce. The Alliance's 1886 platform even included a call for legislation banning agricultural futures and land speculation.

Growing rapidly as drought intensified the underlying economic conditions driving farmers into debt and farm tenancy, the Texas Alliance claimed over 100,000 members by 1886 (and some 200,000 by 1890). However, as with the Greenback Party before it, internal disputes among the movement's leaders over whether to stress political reform or self-help undermined its success. Many of the Alliance's more conservative members were troubled by the seeming shift toward third-party revolt implicit in the movement's 1886 platform. They argued instead for the creation of rural cooperatives, a statewide Alliance exchange to buy surplus crops, and political backing for the reformist wing of the Democratic Party under the leadership of Attorney General (later Governor) James S. Hogg. More radical members of the Alliance, however, distrusted Hogg and the Democrats and soon grew disenchanted with the movement's failure to push for more extreme political reforms. Hence, while still numerically powerful as the 1880s came to a close, the Alliance grew increasingly irrelevant as its conservative members backed the Democrats and its more radical members shifted their allegiance to a new reform effort: Populism.

Populism integrated elements of all the reform movements that came before it. Built on a core of the more radical membership of the Texas Alliance and other similar groups, Populism not only claimed the most members of any of the nineteenth century's rural-based reform efforts but also posed a real and substantial threat to the Democratic Party's control of Texas. Whereas the reform Democrats under Hogg shared many of the same objectives as the Populists — among them railroad regulation, laws forbidding the granting of land to foreign corporations, and antitrust legislation outlawing business practices in restraint of trade — they balked at some of the Populists' more radical objectives. Most important among these were government ownership of railroads, the abolition of the national banking system, the creation of an income tax, the imposition of an eight-hour workday, and the development of a subtreasury system that would issue agricultural loans in the form of tickets (based on crop yields) that could be used as legal tender (i.e., as paper money). Unlike calls for corporate regulation or limits on government indebtedness, these proposals directly attacked private control of the economy — capitalism itself. Although the Democrats could and would adopt many of the more reformist aspects of the Populists' agenda — including even the call for inflation by the free coinage of silver — they could not, and would not, accept the frontal attack on capitalism represented by the attack on national banks and the subtreasury plan. This was not reform. This was revolution.

In truth, Populism was at its heart largely a call for class-based warfare. Populists urged have-nots to use the power of government to wrest power and control away from the haves; they urged small farmers to attack city-based merchants and large planters who controlled agricultural markets condemning them to poverty; they urged nativists to attack the perceived foreign elements who seemed to be imposing unwanted changes on the South. True, the means for launching this attack was the structure of direct popular democracy — that is to say, in response to the explicit wishes of the majority via such approaches as the direct election of senators, the referendum and recall, and the adoption of the Australian (secret) ballot. However, given that the Populists thought of themselves as "the people," their call for participatory democracy was little more than a demand that government assault the causes of *their* problems and make *their* lives better.

In Texas, Populism was the product of forty years of agricultural discontent. By the 1890s, Texas farmers were desperate. They needed help and help now. Whereas the more successful farmers were satisfied with the Democrats' more limited reforms, the truly downtrodden required — and demanded — something more. Populism and its call for the economic redistribution of wealth by government action provided that something more, and poor farmers across the state — tenants, sharecroppers, and even landowners — gave the party their support.

Joining the ranks of the Populist movement were the state's many poor black farmers. Rural poverty affected black Texans even more than it did white. By the 1890s, a full three-fourths of black farmers were tenant farmers, the vast majority trapped in the most destructive form of tenancy, sharecropping. Even worse off were those black Texans working as agricultural day laborers. Although most black Texans still aligned themselves with the Republican Party, many were drawn to the message of rural reformism promoted by the Farmers' Alliance and other movements. Since the mid-1870s, reformers within the black community had organized colored reform associations in counties across the state. In 1886, the Colored Farmers' Alliance of Texas, ultimately claiming some ninety thousand members, formed as a mirror organization to the all-white Farmers' Alliance. With the arrival of Populism, these organizations and their membership joined white farmers in shifting their allegiance to the new third party.

Populists were going to need this support. Early in the party's history, its leaders understood that, without the support of the state's black voters, victory was unlikely. As one black delegate to the state's first Populist convention noted: "The negro will be the balancing vote in Texas." Allying with black Texans, however, posed significant dangers. Race hatred and discrimination were still alive and strong in the hearts and minds of Texas whites. Many within the new party distrusted black voters, and few were willing to espouse social equality between the races even as they sought black votes. Party leaders also feared the potential for a more general white backlash against the party's biracial composition. Still, staying in the Democratic Party meant muting the more radical aspects of their reform agenda; given the Populists' more radical aims, merger with the Democrats was a risk that the party leadership did not want to take.

In this instance, need outweighed hate. Although with internal grumbling, Texas Populists had by the early 1890s welcomed blacks into their ranks. In Gonzales County, blacks constituted one-third of the party's membership and six of the nineteen members of the county delegation attending the party's 1892 state convention. In Colorado County, black party membership stood at half, with two of the three county chairmen being black. Statewide, comparable numbers existed wherever blacks made up appreciable portions of the county electorate. At the same time, the black Texan J. B. Rayner of Calvert served on the party's state Executive Committee. The party's 1892 platform even included a call for "equal justice and protection under the law to all citizens, without reference to race, color or nationality."

Backed by African American votes, the Populists soon began to show remarkable — if still not fully victorious — electoral results. In 1892, the Populist gubernatorial candidate Thomas L. Nugent received over 100,000 votes in his losing effort against the incumbent, Hogg. In other contests, six Populist candidates won seats to the state house of representatives and one to the state senate. Populists also gained office in local elections across the state. Two years later, Nugent gained over 150,000 votes for governor, losing this time by only some 56,000 votes. Meanwhile, Populist candidates won twenty-two state house of representatives races and two state senate races. In the bitter 1896 gubernatorial election, Jerome J. Kearby, running as a fusion candidate for the Populist and Republican Parties, amassed

238,000 votes against Democrat Charles A. Culberson's 298,000 — the Populist share of the vote total amounting to 44 percent. On the national scene, the Populist ticket for president won 32 percent of the votes cast by Texans.

By the 1890s, Populism not only stood a chance of winning real power in Texas but actually seemed to be on the verge of doing so. Add in the party's electoral success elsewhere in the South — in 1894, a combined Populist-Republican ticket won power in North Carolina — and the possibility of a Populist victory in Texas seemed all too likely. A few more votes, one way or another, and the agrarian dream of economic and social reform would be a reality.

This turn of events could not have come at a worse time for the Democrats. Far from being a cohesive movement, the Texas Democratic Party of the 1890s was at war with itself. Since the late 1880s, moderate reformers led by Governor Hogg had been battling conservative Democrats led by the former state attorney general, George Clark, for control of the party. In 1890, the reformers won. As governor, Hogg implemented what became known as the "Hogg Laws," a series of legal reforms that included the law founding the Texas Railroad Commission; laws forcing land corporations to sell off their holdings in fifteen years and prohibiting further grants to foreign corporations in an effort to get the land into the hands of citizen settlers; and a law restricting the amount of bonded indebtedness by county and municipal government. In 1892, reacting to these reforms, anti-Hogg Democrats led by Clark bolted the party, backing Clark as an independent candidate for governor. Hogg's victory over Clark (by just under sixty thousand votes) ended the conservative breakaway movement. Still, disputes between the two branches of Democrats over policy — and leadership — continued through the decade.

Deeply concerned that the combination of Populism's biracial appeal and the internal disorder wracking the Democratic Party might lead to a Populist victory, the Democratic leadership responded aggressively to the Populist threat. First, it sought to rebuild party unity within the state. In March 1894, leaders from each faction met in a "Harmony Meeting" in Dallas and agreed to put aside — for a time — old differences and work for the party's common good. Differences still remained (many of them significant and long lasting), but, facing the prospect of a Populist-Republican victory in 1894 or 1896, Texas

Democrats of all stripes closed ranks. With harmony in the party restored, Texas Democrats set out to lessen Populism's appeal by embracing the more moderate aspects of the Populist reform agenda as their own. They therefore called for increased government regulation of business, antitrust prosecutions of interstate corporations, and electoral reform. At the same time, the national Democratic Party adopted a reform agenda incorporating other less radical aspects of Populist tenets (in this case emphasizing inflation via the unlimited coinage of silver) and nominated the reformer William Jennings Bryan as its presidential candidate on this reform platform.

The Democrats' adoption of part of the Populists' agenda, combined with Bryan's nomination, placed the Populists in an uncomfortable and largely untenable position. They could respond in one of two ways, neither of them appealing. Either Populists could join the Democrats to help bring about a Bryan victory, in the process achieving at least *some* of their political objectives, or they could remain true to their objectives and run their own candidate for president, but at the cost of assuring a Republican victory by splitting the reformist vote. Both options were unpalatable. Supporting Bryan meant abandoning the rest of their political demands and undermining their organizational cohesion as a separate party. Yet going it alone meant facing the real prospect of meeting none of their political goals at all.

Torn between two distasteful options, the Texas Populists split their decision. On the national level, they threw in with Bryan and the Democrats (although with serious reservations and even discord on the part of many skeptical Texas Populists). Choosing victory over ideology, they decided to sacrifice the more extreme components of their reform agenda. If Bryan won, they won; if he lost, they lost. Hence, although the party sought to retain its separate identity, nominating Bryan as a *Populist* candidate for president rather than merging with the Democrats, in terms of the *national* election the two parties effectively became one. By contrast, on the *state* level, Texas Populists scorned the Texas Democrats' moderate reform agenda and allied with the Republicans to run Jerome J. Kearby against the Democrat Charles A. Culberson for governor. All too familiar with the moderate aims of the reform Democrats, they held out for total victory or defeat.

In the end, neither approach worked to the Populists' advantage. Nationally, in a hard-fought, bitter campaign, Bryan lost the election to the Republican William McKinley, who convinced a majority of voting Americans that the Populist-inspired Democratic reforms threatened prosperity and economic growth. Texas endured an equally hard and bitter campaign, one in which, in county after county, local election management was marred by levels of fraud, intimidation, and outright violence against Populist voters not seen since the end of Reconstruction. In the end, the Populist-Republican candidate narrowly lost to the Democrat. Here, too, victory came because the winner was able to convince enough voters that the other side's makeup and reform agenda was too radical and dangerous to trust. In particular, the Democrats were able to turn the Populists' high level of African American support (made greater by their fusion with the black-dominated Republican Party) against them, playing the race card and luring the more conservative and racist voters away from the fusion ticket. In the end, the Populists were sixty thousand votes short of victory.

This twin defeat proved fatal to the Populist movement. Although Texas Populists would run candidates in the next two elections, their moment had passed. Organizationally and emotionally devastated by their defeat in both the presidential and the gubernatorial elections, Populists across the state lost interest in politics. Some, disgusted, abandoned politics altogether. Others, confused by the Populists' on-again, off-again merger with the Democrats, returned to the Democratic fold. Most wondered how victory had eluded their grasp.

Meanwhile, buoyed by their victory at home, but devastated by their loss nationally, Texas Democrats also entered a period of change and introspection. With the Populist threat declining, the party's conservative forces went on the offensive. Although the reformer Culberson would win reelection in 1896, the next two governors, Joseph D. Sayers and Samuel W. T. Lanham, were members of the party's conservative wing. Each, in turn, abandoned the party's reform efforts. Thereafter, the goal was to maintain power and do nothing that might upset the party's political dominance and unity — a goal that the party's more reform minded members found frustrating yet impossible to defeat.

It was during this period of conservative resurgence within the Democratic Party and continuing disintegration of the Populists that the move toward disenfranchisement began. Although separated into many competing and warring factions — conservative and reformist Democrats, white and black former Populists, black and white Republicans — Texans agreed that the political process in their state was defective. Wracked by class warfare, immobilized by political infighting, stricken with political apathy and even disdain, and undermined by extensive electoral fraud and violence (granted, most implemented by the Democrats in their efforts to undermine Populism), Texas politics was a mess. The question was how to fix it.

Whereas many conflicting answers to this question were proposed in the years that followed, one common theme emerged. With the exception of African American voters and a few die-hard Populists, all the parties agreed — whatever their other proposals for change — that some form of disenfranchisement had to be part of the solution. Voting in Texas needed reform, and, in the eyes of many, the first step to reform was making sure that only the "right" voters were allowed access to the polls. Of course, what constituted the right voters was open to debate. Members of the competing factions within Texas politics all had their own ideas on the subject. Yet, whatever the details of their vision of a purified electorate, each saw advantage — both generally and to themselves — in shrinking the electorate.

For reform Democrats (now organized as Progressives), power within the party depended on convincing former Populists to return to the Democrats. Presumably, given their more radical past, the former Populists would join the reform Democrats and, thus, help return the reformers to leadership of the party. The problem was how to convince the former Populists not just to return to the party but to do so as allies of the Progressives. Populism, after all, had been largely a rejection of the Hogg Democrats' more moderate reform aims. One area of agreement between the two sides, however, was electoral reform. Each decried the corruption and fraud endemic to the existing political process. Electoral reform, in other words, could be a path by which aggrieved former Democrats returned to the party. Not surprisingly, then, the Progressive Democrats pushed disenfranchisement as an electoral reform designed to prevent fraudulent voting and to keep the purchasable voter from the polls.

For the former Populists, disenfranchisement appealed as the logical outgrowth of electoral reform. Cleaning up the voting process had been a major component of the Populists' reform agenda. Direct election of senators (who, before the Seventeenth Amendment [1913], were still chosen by state legislatures), popular participation in the legislative process by means of the ballot initiative and recall, and the imposition of a secret ballot to assure sincere and honest voting all aimed at increasing the openness and accessibility of the political process. The goal was to break the power of political bosses and professional politicians by removing the endemic fraud and vote buying common in Texas elections — which the Populists blamed, in large part, as the source of their twin defeats in the 1896 election. Disenfranchisement, offered by reform Democrats as a purifying process, seemed to fit this pattern. Voting by such other groups as blacks and especially Mexican Americans was correctly seen as the source of conservative bosses' power. Drive such debased voters from the polls, and the remaining pure voters (by which the former Populists meant themselves) could clean up politics and fix Texas's many problems. Of course, this reasoning ignored the likelihood that disenfranchisement would target poor whites as well as blacks — but, for many Populists, race hate, limits in the disenfranchising techniques proposed, and general political exhaustion screened this effect from view.

Many Populists also found disenfranchisement appealing because it offered them a means to take their revenge. Their alliance with Texas blacks had been based, as the historian C. Vann Woodward describes it, on "want and poverty, the kinship of a common grievance and a common oppressor." Blacks were welcomed into the party because they were "in the ditch just like we [were]," not out of any deep-seated egalitarianism on the part of white Populists. With the movement's defeat, the kinship of need ended — and with its end came fingerpointing and denunciation. Had blacks not been a part of the movement, many former Texas Populists argued, the Democrats' race baiting would not have worked, and the party would have won. Consequently (if illogically), any negative fallout from disenfranchisement and electoral reform was simply the black community's own fault for failing Populism. In any case — and for any reason — as far as many Populists were concerned, an end to black voting would be a good thing. Any plan that would bring it about had their support.

Interestingly, Conservative Democrats were the least interested in shrinking the electorate. The Populists' understanding of the sources of conservative boss rule in Texas was, in fact, accurate. Blocking voting by controlled or bought voters maintained the bosses' control of Texas politics. This was especially the case among the powerful Anglo bosses of South Texas, each of whose power was built on control of the Mexican American vote. For years, these bosses and their allies in the legislature had derailed all efforts to limit the vote. A poll tax was first proposed — and defeated by conservative Democrats — in the state's constitutional convention of 1875, efforts to impose it arising again in 1879, 1881, 1883, and throughout the 1890s. As late as 1899, a poll tax amendment failed to garner the necessary two-thirds vote for passage.

Yet, as the new century dawned, even these bosses realized the advantages inherent in a smaller electorate. Whereas the Populists might ignore the race-neutral aspects of the poll tax, the bosses clearly saw the impact that disenfranchisement would have on the poor *white* electorate. Given the support that poor white voters had given to Populism, not to mention the likelihood that, with no other choices, poor whites would switch their allegiance to the reform wing of the Democrats, excluding poor white farmers from the polls could only be to the conservatives' ultimate benefit. Besides, smaller numbers of voters would, in fact, make it easier to win elections with their controlled minority-based voters (even shrunk as they were going to be as a result of the poll tax) because the *total* number of votes necessary for victory would shrink as well.

By the early twentieth century, then, all these forces combined to reform the electoral process in Texas by passing an annual, noncumulative poll tax of $1.50 (plus local and/or county surcharges) per voter — the payment of which was a precondition of voting. Although even back then $1.50 was not a huge amount, the extensive poverty in Texas (where, for many, yearly profits could be counted in the single digits) meant that paying $1.50 or more for the questionable right to vote was a luxury that few could afford. The result was a massive decline in the number of registered voters across the state — which, combined with the abandonment of their franchise by voters disgusted with the electoral process, shrunk the numbers of Texas voters dramatically.

Before the poll tax's adoption in 1902, for instance, white voting rates stood well above 60 percent — 88 percent in 1896, 80 percent in 1900, and 62 percent in 1902. With the poll tax, however, only 46 percent of white voters went to the polls in 1904. This dramatic reduction was followed by a voting rate of just 27 percent of eligible voters in the next election. And, although in 1908 the percentage of white voters would increase to 30 percent, it dropped back two years later to a mere 29 percent. Not even the all-important Democratic primary could generate more than about a 40 percent turnout, even in the highly contested gubernatorial elections of 1908 and 1910.

Massive in scope, and immediate in its impact, the decline in the size of the voting electorate had an unintended consequence, however: the empowerment of black voters. The shrinking of the number of potential voters magnified the influence of small numbers of swing voters — foremost among whom were black Texans. This was especially the case in the all-important Democratic primary (which, since it excluded Republican and third-party voters, had an even smaller pool of potential voters than that found in the general election). True, 1902's imposition of the poll tax had significantly affected black voting rates. With over three-quarters of them trapped in the poverty of tenant farming and sharecropping, most Texas blacks were effectively disenfranchised by the poll tax. (Of course, the combination of fraud, intimidation, and outright violence that had accompanied the defeat of Populism had already driven many from the polls, but, in terms of its subsequent impact, the outcome was the same.)

Still, *most* did not mean *all*. Scattered across the state, and especially in the cities, a sizable number of black Texans had the resources to pay the poll tax and vote. Where elections were close — as was often the case in Democratic primaries — these few black votes could be key in shaping the election's outcome. As the historian Forrest G. Wood notes, Texas blacks "did not need a numerical majority in order to enjoy a political majority. Rather, if the total number of eligible Negro voters was greater than the difference in the number of votes cast for each [candidate], the Negroes had a 'majority.'"

The potential of black (and, in South Texas, Mexican American) votes to swing a Democratic primary was well-known. For years, where elections had been close, desperate white politicians had turned to the black community for help. As the historian William Brophy notes: "An outstanding characteristic of the Negro vote in the late nineteenth century was the extent to which it was manipulated. . . . The black vote was purchasable." In some counties, such as Bexar, established political bosses viewed black votes as a resource to enhance their power, often paying the poll taxes of poor black and Hispanic voters out of their own pockets in return for their votes. In other counties, such as Fort Bend, the working-class factions of the white Democrats — known there as the Woodpeckers — turned to blacks as allies in their ongoing class conflict with elite white landowners (organized as the Jaybirds). In either case, the poll tax's shrinking of the electorate only magnified this tendency.

It was in the context of these disputes within the white community that efforts to exclude blacks from the Democratic Party arose. With forty-plus years of political turmoil under their belts, Texas Democrats found themselves being drawn into a new round of factional infighting — only now with the added complication that black voters often cast the deciding votes. Given most white Democrats' racial views and their general exhaustion with political infighting, this was an unacceptable situation. Yet, in the partisan drive to win, factions within the Democratic Party ranks were reaching out to black voters — and would do so in the future as conditions dictated.

White Democrats, in other words, turned to the AWP in large part because they could not trust themselves *not* to make use of the forbidden fruit of black votes — at least when those votes meant the difference between victory and defeat. The AWP, however, removed the temptation by removing the votes. As North Carolina's widely read white-supremacist paper the *Raleigh News and Observer* noted on February 4, 1899 (quoting its editor, Josephus Daniels), without an AWP, "divisions among white men might result in bringing about a return to the deplorable conditions when one faction of white men called upon the negroes to help defeat another faction." Drive blacks from the primaries, however, and the result was, to white Democratic eyes, a much neater electoral process. As the *News and Observer* concluded: "When the negro vote is eliminated, a nomination by the party of the white men is equivalent to election." That it also meant that blacks would be denied a voice in the governing process was simply a side benefit — welcome and much appreciated, but a side benefit nonetheless.

The idea of a race-limited primary was not new to Texas. As early as 1876, whites in Harrison County organized the White Citizen's Club to wrest power from the black-led Republicans. Employing fraud and intimidation, the club took control of county government in 1878. Twelve years later, it solidified its control of local politics, adopting a resolution seeking to limit participation in primary elections to white men only.

In later years, periodic efforts to overwhelm black voting (especially in counties with large black populations) led local whites to organize similar "white men's parties." Most limited their efforts to informal intimidation and fraud. The turmoil associated with the rise of the Populist Movement in the 1890s changed this trend, however. Organized in 1888, for example, the all-white Fort Bend County Jaybird Club (later the Jaybird Democratic Association) began running a white-only preprimary in the early 1890s. Participation in the "Jaybird primary" was predicated on a pledge to support the winners in the upcoming Democratic Party primary. Failure to abide by this pledge, in turn, meant social and political isolation. The Matagorda County White Man's Union held a separate, white-only primary in September 1894 to choose candidates to run in the general election against the Democratic and Republican nominees. One month later, whites in Brazoria County organized a similar white citizens' ticket (known as the Tax Payer's Union) for the upcoming election. Waller County whites adopted the same strategy in 1893, while Marion County whites did not organize their AWP (which they implemented by the simple expedient of threatening blacks with violence as they neared the polls) until 1897. In 1898, the Bell County Democratic Executive Committee adopted a new strategy to create an AWP, a mandatory pledge for primary voters that began: "I am a white democratic voter. . . ." Soon thereafter, Democrats in Grimes County organized their own White Man's Union whose charter limited membership, and, hence, the right to vote in the union's preprimary, to whites only. By 1900, the combination of an all-white preprimary and race-based violence gave the union complete control of the county. And so the trend spread across the state. Its coverage, however, was spotty. Hence the perceived need for a statewide approach.

The first step in adopting a statewide AWP came in 1903. Following passage of the poll tax amendment in 1901, and before its implementation in 1902, state legislators took up other aspects of electoral reform. Among them were calls for new rules mandating that the parties replace the practice of using conventions to nominate political candidates with the more "democratic" practice of direct primaries. The idea was to democratize the nomination process, now that the electorate had been purified by the poll tax. Of course, given that blacks and other minority groups still could vote (although now in small numbers), just how pure the electorate had become was open to debate. Hence the need for further reform.

Leading the call for reform was Representative A. W. Terrell. An ally of former Governor Hogg and his reform Democrats, Terrell long had supported franchise limits. As Terrell explained in 1906: "Whether universal manhood suffrage is good for the country depends entirely on the sort of men who vote." Let the wrong type of men vote — "the thriftless, idle and semi-vagrant element of both races" — and chaos was the sure result. To Terrell, laws and constitutional provisions such as the Fifteenth Amendment that permitted anyone to vote were "the political blunder[s] of the century." To this end, Terrell had introduced legislation in support of poll taxes as early as 1879. Now, with the passage of the poll tax, Terrell turned his attention to better regulating primaries.

Proposed in 1902, and adopted in 1903, the Terrell Election Law, as it came to be known, was a series of related reform measures. Among these measures were rules outlining the use of primaries to choose candidates for the general election; mandatory declaration by voters of their party membership in order to vote; the use of official ballots; and the requirement that all poll taxes be paid between October and February, a full six months before the primaries and nine months before the general election. (The idea was that, by separating the payment of poll taxes from the election, poor voters either would forget to pay so far in advance of the election or would lose their receipts and, thus, be barred from voting.) Although some of the changes that Terrell implemented were improvements over the old ad hoc process of choosing candidates, the explicit objective behind these measures was, not reform, but the exclusion of poor, and especially minority, voters. When one legislator attempted to amend Terrell's bill to allow payment of poll taxes by a third party, for instance, Terrell rejected the idea, arguing: "It would open the flood gates for illegal voting as one person could buy up the Mexican and Negro votes." On the other hand, Terrell supported an amendment proposed by Thomas B. Love of Dallas that allowed (presumably racist) county executive committees of each party to "prescribe further qualifications" for voting in the primary as they felt necessary. If all else failed, the law's champions reasoned, party officials could keep blacks out. Thus, although the Terrell Election Law never directly mentioned blacks, its supporters saw it as a direct bar to African American voting in Democratic Party primaries. Their expectation was that local party executives across the state would quickly adopt rules limiting participation in the primary to whites only.

On the whole, this proved to be an accurate prediction. Following the law's enactment, most county Democratic Party boards promptly adopted rules excluding blacks. For many, these rules merely codified the status quo. Still, not every Democratic leader approved of the new law and its requirements. In many counties and cities, taxpaying blacks could still vote in Democratic primaries, and Democratic candidates continued to solicit their votes. In Beaumont, for instance, one local paper estimated that, during the 1904 primary, over five hundred people ignored the new election law's implied limits. Meanwhile, in the Rio Grande Valley, Democratic bosses evaded the new law by the simple expedient of defining Mexican American voters as white.

Troubled by the failure of some Democrats to abide by the exclusionary intent of his law, Terrell took up the issue of primaries again in 1905. To halt the practice of bought votes, the new law made it a misdemeanor to pay someone else's poll tax. It also required that all parties polling over 100,000 votes in the last election (which included only the Democrats) *had* to use primaries to pick their candidates. The law then gave to each party's county executive committees the power to determine membership eligibility and, hence, to determine who could vote in its primaries. Given that, just one year earlier, the state Democratic Executive Committee had "suggested" that county committees adopt the pledge "I am a white person and a Democrat" as a prerequisite to voting in the primary, and given also Terrell's long history as an opponent of black voting, the 1905 law's discriminatory intent was clear and effective. While some county executives still refused to exclude minority voters, most now fell into line.

In later years, the state legislature would fiddle regularly with the election laws. Among subsequent changes were rules allowing women to vote in primary elections, rules imposing uniform standards for the use of party loyalty oaths, and a series of amendments that defined the runoff process when no candidate received a majority of the votes in a primary election (a common occurrence when primaries, such as those run by the Democrats, drew more than two candidates). Yet at no time did anyone directly challenge the general tenor and/or disenfranchising approach of the Terrell law. Except in a few counties that continued to allow co-opted African American voting in primary elections (and the many cities that, because of the general use of nonpartisan voting, remained open to qualified voters of all races), blacks and other minorities were effectively disenfranchised. Denied access to the one election that determined who ultimately would win political office, Texas blacks now were powerless to affect public policy. They could and would vote in the general election, and some even managed to vote in a Democratic primary, but these were essentially meaningless acts.

Yet even this result was not enough for Texas whites. With the end of the First World War, pressure grew for the total exclusion of blacks from the Democratic Party. Although the number of blacks able to vote stood only in the low tens of thousands — and the number of blacks able to vote in Democratic primaries probably stood in the mere hundreds — this was not good enough for white Texans. Exclusion had to be complete.

Exactly why the 1920s saw this revival of race hatred and violence is hard to say. Part of the answer lay in the heightened emotion and stress caused by the First World War. Trapped by the hysteria created by wartime panic and overt nationalistic enthusiasms, a number of minority groups — among them immigrants from Eastern Europe, political radicals, and African Americans — faced discrimination and outright repression from both public and private agencies. With the war's abrupt end, these fierce feelings needed an outlet. On the national level, this need helped spur an epidemic of anti-Communist hysteria known as the Red Scare. In the South, along with anti-Communist concerns, more traditional race-based fears served this purpose. The result was a rise in race hatred represented by the rebirth of the Ku Klux Klan, which, for a short time in the 1920s, attracted tens of thousands of members and came to dominate regional politics.

Another factor was the key influence that those few blacks able to vote in a Democratic primary often had had in close contests. Although the numbers of blacks voting were small, in a close race these few votes could make the difference between victory and defeat. Such was the case in Bexar County's 1918 primary for district attorney, where the candidate John Tobin reached out to San Antonio's black community for votes in a successful effort to win a very close race. Angered by his loss, Tobin's opponent, D. A. McAskill, complained bitterly about Tobin's use of the black vote, noting: "The Democratic Party was ruined unless something was done to protect it." Victorious in the next primary, McAskill again faced an opponent seeking to harness the black vote in 1922. Warning white voters of the "direful domination of local government . . . by the colored people" if blacks were allowed to vote in the Democratic primary, McAskill argued that "any white man who would ask black folk for their votes was not a Democrat." Although successful in his reelection campaign, an angry McAskill now set out to suppress black voting, lobbying the Texas legislature for a law barring blacks from the Democratic primary. Joined by other Texas politicians who feared the influence that black voters might have in a close race, McAskill's project received a warm welcome.

Finally, the courts also influenced the decision by the white Texas political elite to slam the door shut on black voting in the primaries. By the early 1920s, the Texas Supreme Court had ruled in a number of cases that, in Texas, political parties were private organizations. These rulings placed the Democratic Party outside the boundaries of the Fourteenth and Fifteenth Amendments because both Amendments were generally understood to limit only "state action" — that is, action by state or local government. They also gave those Democrats wishing to intensify enforcement of the AWP confidence that their actions would be upheld in the courts as constitutional. Adding to Democrats' sense of comfort, in 1921 the U.S. Supreme Court held in *Newberry v. United States* that primary elections were *not* part of the election process regulated by the civil rights amendments.

Whatever the cause, the result was that, in 1923, the Texas legislature revised the state's primary-election law once again — this time expressly prohibiting, *as a matter of state law*, black voting in the Democratic primaries. As amended, the new statute read in part:

All qualified voters under the laws and constitution of the State of Texas who are bona fide members of the Democratic party, shall be eligible to participate in any Democratic party primary election, provided such voter complies with all laws and rules governing party primary elections; *however, in no event shall a negro be eligible to participate in a Democratic party primary election held in the State of Texas, and should a negro vote in a Democratic primary election, such ballot shall be void and election officials are herein directed to throw out such ballot and not count the same.* (emphasis added)

This statute meant that, thereafter, the Democratic Party was a white party, and that was that. Blacks were neither wanted nor welcome in the party. If this exclusion meant that blacks were, thus, excluded from the forming of public policy, so be it. Texas could not — would not — accept a racially mixed political process. And, until someone did something to change the law, this was the state of politics in Texas.

In fact, as the 1923 law went into effect, just such a campaign to force change was getting under way. Led by the National Association for the Advancement of Colored People, and supported by the entire Texas black community, the fight to defeat the Texas AWP was about to begin.

# CHAPTER 3

# A Rising Tide of Protest

## Early Efforts to Combat
## the Texas All-White Primary

By the second decade of the twentieth century, the situation for Southern blacks was dire. The road to full inclusion in American society that Reconstruction had seemed to open was now closed, with law, entrenched political power, and the white community's prejudice combining to deny African Americans citizenship and even personhood. Segregation — legal separation of the races in all aspects of public life under the specious standard of "separate but equal" — was now the law, and brutal reality, across the South. In Texas, the combination of the poll tax and the all-white primary (AWP) had largely met the Democratic Party's exclusionary objectives — effectively barring Texas blacks from having any say in public policymaking.

Despite these difficulties, and perhaps even because of them, Texas blacks did not give up. For a fleeting moment, they had experienced the wonder of full enfranchisement, and they were not going to accept its denial without a fight. The question was, How? How could Texas blacks fight the AWP? What strategies would work best? Where would the funding for such a campaign come from? And, most important of all, who would lead this fight?

Into this situation came the National Association for the Advancement of Colored People (NAACP). Organized in 1909 by prominent black and white reformers, the NAACP defined its primary objective to be the enlargement of the ongoing struggle for African American civil and political liberty. Strategically, it chose litigation as the technique most likely to bring the quickest results. Conceptually, its goal was to end race-based discrimination — all forms of discrimination — wherever it existed. Practically, its expectations were much smaller — to begin a process that ultimately would defeat segregation and racial oppression.

The drive began as early as 1910, when NAACP lawyers joined the defense team for Pink Franklin, a black farmhand in Orangeburg, South Carolina, who had been arrested for killing a white constable — although, at the time of the incident, Franklin had not realized that the man was a police officer. Franklin was convicted and sentenced to death by an all-white jury. On appeal, the NAACP lawyers argued to the U.S. Supreme Court that the jury's racial imbalance invalidated its verdict. The Supreme Court disagreed, upholding Franklin's conviction.

Defeat did not deter the NAACP, however. Over the next few years, NAACP lawyers brought suit in a number of matters — winning many important cases, although, in the end, failing to achieve the ultimate goal of ending Jim Crow segregation. In 1915, for instance, NAACP President Moorfield Storey filed an amicus curiae (*amicus curiae* is law Latin for "friend of the court," i.e., interested third party) brief on behalf of the NAACP with the Supreme Court in *Guinn v. United States* (a suit to declare unconstitutional Oklahoma's "grandfather" statute, which permitted illiterate whites, but not blacks, to vote). In 1917, Storey argued the case of *Buchanan v. Warley*, successfully challenging residential segregation in Louisville, Kentucky, as an illegal infringement of property owners' right to sell their property freely. In 1926, the NAACP suffered a setback when the Court ruled in *Corrigan v. Buckley* that restrictive covenants (deed restrictions that limited a property owner's right to sell his property, e.g., to nonwhites or Jews) were constitutional because they were mere private agreements falling outside the reach of the civil rights amendments. However, three years earlier, in *Moore v. Dempsey*, Storey convinced the Court that murder trials carried on in the heat of public passion and showing clear race prejudice could constitute denials of due process of law under the Fourteenth Amendment.

As part of this litigation strategy, the NAACP's lawyers set their sights on the Texas AWP. They chose the AWP for two important reasons. First, they recognized the intrinsic importance of voting as a means of enhancing African American civil rights. Give blacks an effective vote, and they would have a tool to pry future gains out of reluctant Southern governments and the white polities that they represented. As the NAACP lawyer William Henry Hastie (a dean of Howard University Law School who later became a federal judge) explained in a 1973 interview with the historian Darlene Clark Hine: "We all felt then that the things we were doing in education or housing or residential segregation and so on, would not amount to much unless the blacks in the South were effectively franchised . . . even though the courts may decide in our favor on any number of those basic and important rights. Unless blacks had the power as voters to influence their local governments, the enforcement of these other rights would be so unsatisfactory that we wouldn't have gained very much by winning those battles." Second, and more significant, the NAACP's lawyers chose the AWP because they felt that rules excluding *registered* voters were more vulnerable to attack than technically race-neutral statutes and constitutional provisions that "just happened" to disallow black voting. This was, in fact, an accurate assumption. In *Breedlove v. Suttles* (1937), for example, the Supreme Court would unanimously uphold Georgia's poll tax, shielding this particular barrier to voting from constitutional attack until the 1960s. Similar Supreme Court rulings in the 1930s and 1940s would affirm literacy tests and would mark the issue of racially gerrymandered districting as a political question beyond the Court's constitutional scope of review. By contrast, the AWP was based on an explicit application of race to deny African Americans the right to vote. This fact made all the difference in the world — or so the NAACP hoped.

The NAACP's lawyers, in other words, saw the AWP, not only as a perfect vehicle for attacking a clear limit on the civil rights of Texas blacks, which it clearly was, but also as an instrument by which to intensify, expand, and solidify their wider aims of dismantling segregation. In this latter regard, the campaign against the AWP stood hand in hand with the NAACP's other assaults on segregated education and the prevailing discriminatory criminal procedures that collectively denied black criminal defendants due process of law. In fact, given the NAACP's commitment to take on only cases that "establish[ed] a precedent which will affect the basic citizenship rights of Negroes and other Americans" (to quote Walter White, NAACP executive secretary from 1931 to 1955), it was mostly in that light that the NAACP's national leadership viewed the fight against the AWP.

In theoretical terms, this big-picture approach made the NAACP lawyers into *repeat players*, to use the term coined by the political scientist Marc Galanter. Repeat players (RPs) are, according to Galanter, individuals or groups who "have many occasions to utilize the courts" in furtherance of a long-term objective. Given this long-term outlook,

RPs have "low stakes" in any single litigation; rather, they seek to "play the odds," pursuing in each litigation tactical advantages by which to further their long-range goals. This pragmatic perspective provides RPs with a number of tactical advantages. One such advantage is the chance to set up particular legal rules or doctrines that, although they might not provide complete victory in the short-run, set the stage for the next legal assault. Another is the experience and expertise that RPs amass from repeated forays into the courts. Having already done it before, RPs can maneuver confidently, clear as to what strategies will or will not work, and capable of using those strategies successfully.

As applied to the actual fight against the AWP, the NAACP's status as an RP afforded its lawyers many of these practical advantages. Foremost among them was the ability to put together a team of skilled litigators — such as NAACP President Moorfield Storey, NAACP Special Counsel Charles Hamilton Houston (1935–1940), and Houston's successor, Thurgood Marshall — who understood, not only the legal issues at hand, but also the politics of using the courts to promote social and political change. As the legal scholar Alan Robert Burch notes: "The Association won victories in the courtroom . . . by exposing how the law discriminated against African-Americans and shaming judges into writing new law." Yet using shame and personal disgust as a motivating tool — or, as Thurgood Marshall once put it, making sure that the judges did not "blind themselves as judges to what they know as men" — was a tricky procedure. Most judges of the day did not want to write new law. The backgrounds and legal training of the vast majority of judges, in fact, argued strongly against such actions. Overcoming this reluctance took tact and a ready knowledge of which buttons — personal, social, and legal — to push to get these judges to act. Give a judge a loophole, no matter how small, and he was likely to take the opportunity to use it to avoid the substantive issue. As RPs, the NAACP's lawyers understood this tendency and, thus, constructed their strategies and arguments to minimize such loopholes and other opportunities for judicial inaction.

Unfortunately, the NAACP's status as an RP also gave rise to many obstacles that would have to be overcome. Foremost among them were the inevitable tensions over questions of strategy and pacing between the NAACP's national leaders and the local black communities that the organization represented in court. The national-office lawyers may have taken the lead in litigating, but they were not alone in carrying out the fight. Behind the strategizing and legal maneuvering lay the concerns, hopes, and dreams of Texas's African American community. At the root, it was their fight, and little could have been done to defeat the AWP without the community's general support. First, the NAACP lawyers needed local residents to serve as litigants. Without a real case or controversy involving a real person experiencing a real harm or loss, federal courts were powerless to act. Yet serving as a named plaintiff in a civil rights suit could be very dangerous. Such litigants faced the significant risk of informal retaliation, whether physical, financial, or social — or so past experience suggested. Second, and in some ways more important, local support served as the engine powering reform. As correspondence between the NAACP's national office and leaders of the Texas black community shows, the drive for ever more intense action in attacking the AWP lay in the hands of those directly affected by this discrimination. Whereas the lawyers may have wanted to act, those denied the vote in Texas *needed* to act, and this difference pushed the lawyers to move faster and to demand more than they might otherwise have wished.

Without the active support of black Texans, then, the NAACP's lawyers were largely powerless to act. Luckily, Texas blacks strongly resented the limits imposed by the AWP, and their relatively large and financially stable urban population gave them the political and economic wherewithal to fight such discrimination. They too understood, as the *Houston Informer* noted in a January 17, 1931, editorial, that "the ballot box is the only thing that carries enough force behind it to bring . . . improvement." For years, black community leaders and newspapers had urged payment of the poll tax and full participation in the general election (despite the limited advantages gained by such participation). Many Texas blacks responded to this call. Scholars estimate that, in 1940, some fifty thousand Texas blacks voted in that year's presidential election. Others went even further, joining civil rights organizations and campaigning for equal rights. The NAACP, in fact, had local chapters claiming thousands of members in cities across Texas.

Unfortunately, such enthusiasm could be as detrimental to careful litigation strategies as it was helpful in generating support for an enfranchisement campaign. The problem was that, although the lawyers from the national office might be RPs, the local chapters of the NAACP and the wider communities that they represented were not. Instead, both groups were what Galanter calls *one shotters*. One shotters (OSs) do not play for long-term goals. For them, the litigation at hand is the most important thing. Winning (judged largely by the practical outcome of the specific litigation) is OSs' goal, not setting some precedent that might lead to some greater gain in the future. This is not to say that OSs do not recognize the potential of a decision to affect more than just the matter at hand. But future concerns were just that, concerns for future cases; OSs want or need victory in the here and now too much to be swayed by such abstract considerations.

In terms of the fight against the AWP, this analysis suggests that, whereas black Texans did not oppose the idea of a broad-based attack on segregation and discrimination and did understand that good things would result from an effective franchise, they had trouble seeing how losing a case (or not making every argument that could help win a case) furthered these ends. After all, without a court victory, there would be no end to the AWP. Where was the advantage in that?

Thus, although the final objective and the specific goals in a court case might be the same — winning a victory that would lead to an end to the AWP — each group had a different idea of what winning involved. For the NAACP lawyers, *how* one gained victory was as important as victory itself; they understood that a win for the wrong reasons could be as damaging as a clear defeat. Black Texans, on the other hand, wanted to vote in the Democratic primary — preferably sooner rather than later — and had trouble seeing how defeat could be preferable to victory.

The first efforts to combat the AWP unfolded within the context of this complex debate over objectives and methods. Whites had effectively excluded blacks from voting in the Texas Democratic primary since the passage of the 1903 Terrell Election Law, which granted all qualified voters in the state the right to vote in any party primary so long as they had successfully completed a prescribed "party test." The law had then allowed any "county executive committee of the party holding any primary election" the right to "prescribe additional qualifications" for participating voters. With no guidelines to limit party action, most Democratic county executive committees had adopted party membership qualifications banning African Americans from voting in the Democratic primary. The effect was the extensive, if not uniform, disenfranchisement of blacks across the state.

At first, black Texans did nothing. While they might not like the AWP, its more negative effects were not immediately apparent. Because most Texas cities had nonpartisan elections (and, hence, held no Democratic primaries from which to exclude black voters), registered blacks could still vote in city, school board, and special-issue elections (such as local options on liquor) with some measure of real impact. There was also the general election, which, although it might not have real meaning in terms of state offices, could have an impact on the national scene. And, in at least some counties, blacks still could vote in the Democratic primaries.

All this changed with the end of World War I and a rebirth of racial animosity and violence within Texas and across the South. Exactly why the 1920s saw this revival of race hatred and violence is hard to say, but revive they did. In terms of black voting, the 1920s brought renewed efforts by white Texans to exclude black voters from all meaningful forms of the franchise.

The battle began in Houston, where, unlike other Texas cities, local Democrats held primary elections for city offices. On January 27, 1921, the Harris County Democratic Executive Committee voted to bar all blacks from the upcoming primary, set to be held on February 9. Before this vote, Houston's registered black Democrats could and did vote in the primary. About this same time, in Bexar County (where, for years, white Democratic politicians had sought black votes), a bitter contest between white politicians led the ultimate victor, D. A. McAskill, to charge that "any white man who would ask black folks for their votes was not a Democrat." Following the election, McAskill began agitating for an end to all black voting in Democratic elections. When McAskill was joined by other angry white voices across the state, the campaign to exclude blacks from the Democratic Party by state law intensified. Reacting to this pressure, the state legislature responded with its updated election law in 1923, ordering "that in no event shall a negro be eligible to participate in a Democratic party primary."

Frustrated and angry, Texas blacks set out to challenge the white primary in the courts, the only forum having the power to change things that was open to them. This was not to say that their chances of winning in the Texas courts (state or federal) were high. The judges who ran these courts were all white Southerners; most were native-born Texans. Each, owing to his vocation as a lawyer and his role as a judge, was almost by definition a member of the state's ruling elite — sharing all the beliefs and biases of that group. And foremost among these beliefs and biases were race distrust and race hatred. Even when a judge wished to overcome these views and support African American civil rights — and often the law's dictates or an appellate opinion would point a judge in this direction — significant pressures stood in the way. For one thing, state judges were elected officials. If they enforced rules at odds with the beliefs of white Texans, their chances of remaining on the bench were slight. And, although federal judges were protected from political pressure by the Constitution's grant of lifetime tenure (assuming good behavior), they still faced significant social pressure, as members of the Southern white elite, to uphold the region's dominant social and political relationships.

The courts, however, were all that black Texans had. They could either turn to the courts or accept political exclusion. They chose to act and hope that the courts — the federal appellate courts, in particular, and the U.S. Supreme Court, above all — would force action.

The first such effort was made by the Houston newspaperman C. N. Love, who, along with other Houston community leaders, filed suit in state district court on February 5, 1921, against the Harris County Democratic Party chairman, James Griffith, and numerous local election judges. Charging that state laws allowing local election boards to prohibit qualified blacks from voting in the Democratic primary violated the Fourteenth and Fifteenth Amendments, Love sought an injunction preventing the defendants from disallowing the votes of Houston blacks in the upcoming primary election. The defendants countered that the 1903 state law permitting local election commissions to prohibit blacks from voting in the Democratic primary (the 1923 law was not yet in force) did not violate the Fifteenth Amendment and that the plaintiffs' complaint, flawed because it included arguments to this end, was inadequate to justify court jurisdiction. State District Judge Charles Ashe fully agreed with this view. He therefore ordered the plaintiffs to submit a new complaint omitting the offending sections. Love and his fellow plaintiffs refused. The

Fifteenth Amendment was the foundation of their case. To remove that argument would destroy their chances of victory. Judge Ashe therefore ordered Love's case dismissed.

Not long after Love brought his suit in state court, Hurley C. Chandler of San Antonio brought a similar action in federal court against the Election Board of Bexar County, this time naming Governor Pat Neff as a defendant as well. As Love had done, Chandler challenged his exclusion under the Fourteenth and Fifteenth Amendments; he too sought an injunction baring enforcement of the law, in this case, the newly passed 1923 election statute. Once again, the defendants argued, first, that the remedy demanded by the plaintiff was beyond the scope of the court to provide and, second, that the new 1923 law did not violate either of the cited amendments. They offered a third argument as well, that "the primary election referred to was not [in fact] an election . . . within the meaning of the Fourteenth and Fifteenth Amendments to the Constitution of the United States." Those amendments, they explained, affected only general elections for political office. Primary elections — by definition held only for selecting candidates for a general election — were different and, hence, did not fall under this prohibition.

Ruling in April 1924, U.S. District Court Judge DuVal West came down foursquare on the defendants' side. As he held, the case raised two questions: (1) Did his court have the power to provide a remedy in this matter under applicable doctrines of equity? (2) Does an act limiting participation in a primary election violate either the Fourteenth or the Fifteenth Amendment? The judge answered both questions no. Paralleling much of the logic followed by the state judge in *Love v. Griffith*, Judge West agreed that, as the event for which the injunction was requested had passed, his court's equity powers did not reach the issue offered for adjudication. On the second question, after a detailed examination of the laws and precedents regulating elections, Judge West ruled: "Generally speaking, a primary election is understood to be one which is limited to qualified electors of a political party, for the purpose of nominating that party's candidates for state or national offices to be voted upon at a future election of the people generally." This being the case, the Texas law was permissible under the Fourteenth and Fifteenth Amendments to the U.S. Constitution.

Defeat in both state and federal courts did not deter the plaintiffs from their objectives. While Chandler chose not to appeal his case, Love pursued an appeal, first to the Texas Court of Civil Appeals, and later to the Texas Supreme Court. Both courts dismissed his appeal on the grounds that, as the election had passed, no actual controversy or injury existed. With no real controversy present, equity jurisdiction (which Love's call for an injunction invoked) could not arise, and neither the Texas Court of Civil Appeals nor the Texas Supreme Court had a case to hear. Persisting, Love and his associates tried to bring their case to the U.S. Supreme Court on a writ of error, charging that the state appellate courts had erred in failing to rule on the merits of the case. Writing for the Court, Justice Oliver Wendell Holmes Jr. affirmed the state courts' positions, however. As the cause of action had ceased to exist, Holmes wrote, "there was no constitutional obligation to extend the remedy beyond what was prayed." Holmes did, however, hold out a ray of hope to Texas blacks: "If the case [had] stood here as it stood before the court of first instance, it would [have] presented a grave question of constitutional law [that the Court] should be astute to avoid hindrances in the way of taking it up."

Holmes's statement in *Love* was what scholars call a *dictum* — a statement by a judge not necessary to the decision of the case before him or her and, thus, having no real legal force. A dictum, however, can provide encouragement to those who seek to guide the law in the direction to which the dictum points. Inspired by Holmes's dictum in *Love* (and ignoring the federal district court's potentially troubling ruling as to the meanings of the words *primary elections* in *Chandler*), the El Paso physician Dr. Lawrence A. Nixon made the next attempt to break the white primary in 1924. At the request of El Paso's NAACP local president, L. W. Washington, Nixon had sought to vote in the July 1924 Democratic primary. Although he was a personal friend of both the election judges, C. C. Herndon and Charles Porras, Nixon was turned away under the state's 1923 election law. "Dr. Nixon," Herndon was said to have exclaimed, "you know we can't let you vote." Herndon and Porras even signed a statement declaring that their *only* reason for turning Nixon away from the polls was his race.

Nixon turned to his personal attorney, Fred C. Knollenberg, for help. He also turned to the national office of the NAACP. Eager to launch a challenge to the AWP, the NAACP agreed to join Nixon's lawsuit, offering Knollenberg $2,500 to argue a case requesting, not only an injunction, but also monetary damages from the election judges. (Knollenberg later noted in a letter to NAACP Executive Secretary Walter White that he never intended to collect such a judgment, "the only object of the suit being to get an adjudication by the Supreme Court of the legal question.") This shift in strategy was an effort to avoid the problem faced by Love and Chandler — namely, the inability of an equity court to provide relief after the fact. While an injunction might have been made moot by the election's passing, damages for past actions were not — or so the NAACP and Knollenberg hoped.

In the U.S. District Court for the Western District of Texas, Nixon's lawyer argued that the 1923 state law was invalid under the Fourteenth and especially the Fifteenth Amendments inasmuch as it "determine[d] the party with which a negro shall affiliate" by excluding a black voter from the Democratic but not the Republican primary. The inevitable result, Knollenberg explained, "deprives him of his rights as an American citizen to determine for himself his choice of parties." This deprivation accordingly made the act a "discriminatory interference with the free exercise of privileges of citizenship and suffrage enjoyed by the plaintiff, together with others of his race, similarly situated and conditioned in the state of Texas."

The defendants responded that the event that Nixon sought to avoid had already occurred and that, therefore, no actual controversy or pending harm existed for the court to prohibit (this despite Nixon's attempt to avoid this ruling on the equity issue with his legal claim for damages). Yet, even if the election were still pending, they continued, "the primary election referred to was not an election within the meaning of the Constitution of the United States." Hence, the Fourteenth and Fifteenth Amendments were not violated. And, in any case, as the matter at hand was "purely a political matter," the court had "no jurisdiction in the matter." End of story.

Judge West agreed with the defendants. Without explanation as to the merits of the case, he dismissed Nixon's petition for the jurisdictional reasons raised by the defendants. This would have been a frustrating result if all Nixon and his lawyers cared about was the trial court's holding — but not if their goal was to launch a litigation that would put the 1923 act under the microscope of appellate constitutional review. Nixon immediately appealed his case to the U.S.

Supreme Court on a writ of error (which the Court granted in the winter of 1926).

At first, things did not go well. Knollenberg was well meaning, but he lacked the expertise to argue his case effectively before the Supreme Court. Even he admitted in a letter to the NAACP head office: "The Court took me to task quite a little." Others were less forgiving. The African American writer James Weldon Johnson, who served as NAACP secretary from 1920 through 1929, commented in a letter that Knollenberg "legally stubbed his toe once or twice." Professor James A. Cobb of Howard University Law School complained that Knollenberg had neither presented the case well nor been as well prepared to argue it as he should have been. Even though the defendants had not bothered to attend the hearing, the confusion generated by Knollenberg's argument of Nixon's case did not bode well for the Court's ultimate ruling.

Luckily, immediately following Knollenberg's oral argument, Texas Attorney General Dan Moody petitioned the Court to allow him to enter the case as a friend of the court and to file an amicus brief. Because he had recently been nominated for the office of governor in an AWP, Moody argued that he had standing to argue in the case before the Supreme Court. The justices agreed, granting Moody's petition, and ordering a rehearing of the case in fifteen days. Worried about his ability to argue the case on the rehearing, Knollenberg wrote to the NAACP board requesting that the NAACP's lawyers "finish it up in such a way that the court will see the Nixon case our way." Accordingly, the NAACP lawyers Arthur Springarn and James Cobb took over the case on rehearing and presented a powerful and convincing case for Nixon's position.

This time, with clear arguments on the record, the outcome was the one that the NAACP desired. Writing for a unanimous Court, Justice Holmes struck down the 1923 Texas voting-rights law as a violation of the Fourteenth Amendment. "It seems . . . hard to imagine a more direct and obvious infringement of the Fourteenth Amendment," Holmes wrote. "While states may do a good deal of classifying that is difficult to believe rational, there are limits [to this power], and it is too clear for extended argument that color cannot be made the basis of a statutory classification affecting the right" to vote in a primary election. Holmes's eloquent opinion, however, did not mention the Fifteenth Amendment or its effect on the AWP. Unwilling to go too fast or too far in reshaping the political reality of the South, Holmes and the other justices refused to address Nixon's Fifteenth Amendment arguments — even though, at the time, and in the view of later scholars, they were far stronger than his Fourteenth Amendment arguments, which the Court adopted. Nor did Holmes address the state's argument that elections under the Fifteenth Amendment referred only to general elections, not to primaries.

Holmes's unwillingness to engage the Fifteenth Amendment raised problems for later voting-rights lawsuits. His opinion for the Court dealt only with the *explicit* prohibition of black voting *by the legislature* as a direct violation of the Fourteenth Amendment's equal protection clause. Would it change things if the legislature were no longer to *impose* the AWP on the Democrats but returned merely to *allowing* the party to impose it on itself? Texas whites quickly asked this question — and answered it yes. Soon thereafter, the newly elected Governor Moody called a special session of the state legislature to amend the primary voting law by deleting every provision that explicitly barred black voting. The legislature did this on June 7, 1927. Once again, the Democratic Party — and the Democratic Party alone — would determine voter qualifications for its primary elections. Not long after the amended law was passed, the Democratic Party Executive Committee resolved: "All white Democrats who are qualified voters under the Constitutions and laws of Texas . . . and none other, [will] be allowed to participate in the primary elections to be [subsequently] held."

Barred once again from voting in the Democratic primary, a number of prominent black Houstonians, led by James Grigsby and Owen DeWalt, set out to challenge the Texas Democratic Party's new ban on black voting. In July 1928, they appeared before Judge Joseph C. Hutcheson Jr. of the U.S. District Court for the Southern District of Texas, seeking a temporary injunction to bar the Executive Committee of the Harris County Democratic Party from hindering qualified black voters in the upcoming primary, in violation of the Fourteenth and Fifteenth Amendments. Primaries existed under the authority of the State of Texas, they argued, which made the party's actions "state action" under the Constitution — an argument designed to get around the state-action limitations of Fourteenth and Fifteenth Amendment constitutional jurisprudence. In line with Holmes's dictum in *Nixon*, the plaintiffs contended that the federal court could not allow a ban on black voting to continue.

Judge Hutcheson disagreed. The state Executive Committee resolution was "purely party action," he held. Although authorized by Texas to run its primaries, the Democratic Party was still a private, voluntary organization, and it could limit its membership as it chose. The ban on joining the Democratic Party therefore posed no "invasion of [the plaintiffs'] legal rights." And, as no legal rights were threatened, the judge concluded, no decision on relief need be made. Hutcheson therefore denied the plaintiffs' request for a restraining injunction.

Stymied, the Houston plaintiffs turned to the NAACP for help in an immediate appeal. The NAACP declined. For one thing, its lead lawyer, Louis Marshall, was unimpressed with the case. He feared that Grigsby's lawyer, R. D. Evans, had failed to emphasize the necessary constitutional points. More to the point, the NAACP had already committed to a second suit by Dr. Nixon in El Paso against the election judge James Condon — a suit that, they felt, made a stronger case (as did Nixon's first suit, *Nixon v. Condon* sought both an injunction and money damages). In fact, to forestall any confusion between the lawsuits, the NAACP lawyers asked Grigsby and DeWalt to drop their planned appeal. After much arm-twisting by the NAACP in the name of race solidarity, Grigsby and DeWalt agreed. Neither man, however, was particularly happy with the NAACP or its litigation strategy. Nor did this result stop other Houston blacks from bringing suits challenging the AWP on their own.

In 1930, for instance, the Houston nightclub owner Julius White sued J. B. "Shorty" Lubbock, Harris County Democratic Party Executive Committee chairman, in state court; White sought an injunction ordering Lubbock to ignore orders from the state Executive Committee to bar blacks from voting. Concurrent with this suit, C. N. Love turned again to the U.S. District Court for the Southern District of Texas for a similar injunction. Citing *Grigsby v. Harris*, both the Texas Court of Civil Appeals and Judge Hutcheson refused the requested writs. As both the state and the federal judges saw matters, until the Supreme Court acted against the AWP, the law was settled.

Not long afterward, *Nixon v. Condon* (1932) resulted in just such a

Supreme Court decision attacking the Texas AWP. The results of *Nixon v. Condon* were mixed, however, as conceptual and doctrinal limits in the Court's ruling gave rise to continued difficulties in the fight against African American disenfranchisement.

Interestingly, the source of this difficulty lay within the black community itself. Tensions between Texas blacks and the NAACP's head office over strategy and pacing had been going on for years. Grigsby, White, and Love each had been represented by three young and aggressive black attorneys, Carter Wesley, J. Alston Atkins, and James Nabrit, all of whom had aspirations to be leaders within Houston's black community. In particular, Wesley, who owned the city's dominant black newspaper, the *Informer*, sought, and would later demand, a leadership role. Frustrated by the slow pace of change under the NAACP's leadership, and convinced that the cause of this failure was the NAACP's exclusive use of white lawyers to argue its cases, Wesley, Atkins, and Nabrit knew that, given the chance, they could do a better job than the NAACP's lawyers. No white lawyer, Wesley argued in his newspaper on July 16, 1932, could "prepare or present Negro cases as well as a trained Negro." More to the point (and this was a point on which all three men strongly agreed), no outsider white lawyer could represent the hopes and dreams of Texas's local black communities. As outsiders and Caucasians, they just did not understand what it meant to be a Texas black denied political power in his own state. *Nixon v. Condon* brought these tensions over conflicting goals to the fore.

Convinced that they had both the evidence and the insight essential to victory in *Nixon v. Condon*, Wesley and Atkins filed an amicus curiae brief with the Court on their own motion and pressured the NAACP's lawyers to allow Wesley or Atkins to take part in oral argument. This request surprised and alarmed the national NAACP. The staff attorney James Marshall noted in a February 1932 letter to Arthur Springarn that he could not "understand what this muddy-minded person [Wesley] is thinking of. He is either abandoning the Constitution or the jurisdiction of the Supreme Court for some point that seems utterly meaningless to me." Marshall, in fact, was more than confused — he was worried. And he had good reason.

In their brief before the Supreme Court, Marshall and his co-counsel, Nathan Margold (both white attorneys from New York City), felt that it was imperative to focus their arguments on a single issue so as not to confuse the Court and not to make it easier for the justices to duck the issues raised by the case. Margold and White's experience as RPs made it clear to them that, given a loophole, the Supreme Court would most likely take it. Fearful that the Court would confine its ruling to the more limited question of the constitutional nature of a primary election, they stressed that "the real issue is not whether a primary election is an election, but whether a vote at such an election is a vote contemplated by the Fifteenth Amendment." They made this argument hoping that the Court would use the Fifteenth Amendment as the means to overturn the AWP. As Marshall and Margold saw it, the Fourteenth Amendment's state-action requirement posed significant dangers to their case. Its equal protection clause was too general to have the sort of directed impact that they hoped a positive ruling in this matter would have. Worse yet, it lent itself all too well to an endless debate over the public versus private nature of the Democratic Party — a debate that, even if unavoidable, they hoped at least to limit. To win, therefore, they were going to have to convince the justices that the Democratic Party was *not* a private agency when it came to primary elections — a goal easier to achieve via the Fifteenth Amendment's more focused reach.

To this end, Marshall and Margold's brief made four central points, each stressing the public function of the Democratic primaries under the Fourteenth and especially the Fifteenth Amendments. First, they argued that the power to exclude African American voters derived *directly* from the 1927 amendments to the 1923 election law, not from any inherent power of the party to choose its own membership arising from its supposed status as a private association. Texas statute had been regulating "every phase of the primary" since 1905, Marshall and Margold noted. How could this be anything but state action? Second, they drew on *Home Telegraph and Telephone Co v. United States* (1913), a U.S. Supreme Court decision that had expanded the scope of the Fourteenth Amendment's state-action requirement to include misconduct by "an officer or other representative of the state." Given that, in *Love v. Wilcox* (1930), the Texas Supreme Court had ruled that the members of the party's Executive Committee were agents of the state with no inherent powers to exclude from the party those Democrats who had voted for the Republicans in the last election, the brief asserted that, under *Home Telegraph*, the Executive Committee's power to exclude African Americans *must* have come from the state as well. The goal here was to create as broad a definition of *state action* as possible so that the state action supporting the AWP could not be defined away by contending that the party's Executive Committee had overstepped the bounds of its statutory authority. Third, they contended that, even if the party had inherent powers to restrict its membership, this particular exclusion was a classification based on race and, hence, constitutionally impermissible under the civil rights amendments. Finally, they noted that state statute directly authorized party election officials; this statutory authorization made them public officials whose conduct could be regulated by the provisions of the Fourteenth and especially the Fifteenth Amendment.

Directly countering most of the Democratic Party's anticipated arguments as to its private nature and, hence, the private nature of its primaries, the NAACP's brief took pains to keep the focus of its arguments on the public nature of the Democratic Party and its primaries. Convince the justices that even one aspect of the election was public, and the AWP would fall — or, at least, Texas would find it difficult to have any primary elections without allowing black voters to take part. Other arguments could have been put forth as to the "wrongness" of the AWP, and those arguments might actually have helped win the case at hand, but they would have taken the focus away from the public nature of primary elections as regulated by the Fifteenth Amendment — to the detriment of future cases. This was an outcome that Marshall and Margold were careful to avoid.

Unfortunately, Wesley and Atkins were not so careful. Concerned with winning the case at hand — which their perspective as OSs led them to view as the paramount goal — and not experienced enough in Supreme Court argument to see the hidden trap in their assertions, not only did they repeat the arguments made by the NAACP lawyers, but they also added arguments directly attacking the Texas Democratic Party *Executive Committee's* imposition of the AWP. In particular, they argued that the party's capacity to choose its members was distinct from the power of the Executive Committee to act on behalf of the party. Inasmuch as the current rule imposing the AWP was the result of a ruling by the Executive Committee, the brief contended that the AWP was invalid and should be overturned. Although an accurate assessment of the legal situation in Texas, this argument took the focus away from state action and the party's effective role as an agent for the state in running primary elections. This was the problem. As the legal scholar Alan Robert Burch notes: "[Atkins and Wesley's] theory of state action made sense only if the goal was merely to win the case at hand. Atkins and Wesley did not appreciate how much they were conceding to the party on the continuum of where to draw the line on state action, nor how difficult it would be to win that ground back later." More to the point, their argument gave the justices a loophole by which to avoid bringing the Texas AWP directly under the Fourteenth and Fifteenth Amendments. It was a loophole that the justices willingly seized.

Justice Benjamin N. Cardozo (who succeeded Justice Holmes in 1932) wrote for the Court. Responding to the NAACP's arguments, Cardozo agreed that, in running primary elections, the Texas Democratic Party was not a simple voluntary association. Its organization and control of these elections derived directly from a "grant of power" from the state and, hence, was a prohibited state action under the Fourteenth Amendment. As constituted, the Texas white primary was unconstitutional. However, as was Holmes in his 1927 opinion attacking the Texas white primary, Cardozo was unwilling to overturn the Texas AWP on the broad constitutional grounds of the Fourteenth Amendment alone. As he noted, in his opinion:

> Whether the effect of Texas legislation has been to work so complete a transformation of the concept of a political party as a voluntary association, we do not now decide. . . . Whatever our conclusion might be if the statute had remitted to the party the untrammeled power to prescribe the qualifications of its members, nothing of the kind was done. Instead, the statute lodged the power in a committee, which excluded the petitioner and others of his race, not by virtue of any authority delegated by the party, but by virtue of an authority originating or supposed to originate in the mandate of the law.

"A narrower base will [therefore] serve for our judgment in the cause at hand," Cardozo concluded. That "narrower base" was the party/Executive Committee distinction proposed by Atkins and Wesley in their brief. "Whatever inherent power a state political party has to determine the content of its membership," Justice Cardozo wrote, "resides in the state convention." Given this fact, Texas's state-action delegation of power in this matter was a delegation to the Executive Committee, not to the party as a whole. And, Justice Cardozo noted in an aside, that body had never declared its "will to bar negroes of the state from admission to the party ranks."

Cardozo's invocation of this fact limited the reach of the Court's decision. "With the problem thus laid bare and its essentials exposed to view," Justice Cardozo concluded, "the case is seen to be ruled by [our 1927 ruling of] *Nixon v. Herndon*. Delegates of the State's power have discharged their official functions in such a way as to discriminate invidiously between white citizens and black. . . . The Fourteenth Amendment, adopted as it was with special solicitude for the equal protection of members of the Negro race, lays a duty upon the court to level by its judgment these barriers of color." To this end, the Texas AWP was an impermissible discrimination under the Fourteenth Amendment. Of course, whether a similar rule from the party membership as a whole would cross the line drawn by the Court in *Nixon v. Condon* was unknown and beyond the scope of the case. This concession changed everything.

On the surface, *Nixon v. Condon* seemed like a sweeping victory for Texas blacks. The Court had declared the Texas AWP unconstitutional under the Fourteenth Amendment. The AWP seemed to be dead. Yet Justice Cardozo's opinion for the Court gave the Texas Democrats a sizable opportunity to step around the Court's ruling and resuscitate the AWP — and that opportunity, ironically, had its roots in the amicus brief filed by Wesley and Atkins. In fact, that brief had laid out for Texas Democrats exactly how to circumvent the Court's ruling. All the party had to do was have the full membership — organized via the state convention — vote to exclude blacks, and the AWP remained in full force (or, at least, in force pending another Supreme Court ruling two or more years in the future). Not surprisingly, Texas Democrats were quick to seize the chance offered to them. Responding to Justice Cardozo's dictum on the state convention's inherent power, on May 24, 1932, the Texas Democratic state convention resolved unanimously: "All white citizens of the State who are qualified to vote under the Constitution and the laws of Texas shall be eligible for membership in the party and as such be eligible for participation in the primaries." In the next primary season, most blacks were once again turned away from the polls. (Confusion over the new law's reach allowed a few blacks in Houston and other cities to vote; however, election officials ultimately threw those votes out.) The AWP was still alive and in full force.

Foiled in their efforts to break the AWP, Wesley and Atkins were unwilling to acknowledge their role in this failure, blaming the NAACP and its reliance on white lawyers to argue their cases. Undaunted, Houston blacks turned once more to the U.S. District Court for the Southern District of Texas for relief, hoping that its new judge, Thomas M. Kennerly, would prove more open to their arguments than had Judge Hutcheson (who had been elevated to the U.S. Court of Appeals for the Fifth Circuit). In part, their hope was vindicated. Given Justice Cardozo's opinion in *Nixon v. Condon*, Judge Kennerly ruled in *White v. County Democratic Executive Committee of Harris County* that "the powers exercised by the [state Democratic] convention in passing such a resolution [banning black voting] were derived from the state of Texas" and, hence, prohibited by the Fourteenth Amendment. "Unlike Moses, who refused to be known as the son of Pharaoh's daughter, the Democratic Party in Texas has over a period of twenty-five years, chosen to be known as a child and agency of the state of Texas, abandoning its own inherent powers, and choosing to conduct its affairs under grants of power from the state." Yet, despite this concession to the right of blacks to vote in the Democratic primary, Kennerly ultimately proved no more willing to act than Judge Hutcheson had been, dismissing the case on the grounds that his Court did not have "jurisdiction to entertain complainant's bill because of the nature of his prayer for relief." In effect, Kennerly explained, the plaintiffs were requesting "a mandamus against respondents to require [the] respondents . . . to allow [blacks] to vote in such primary." Although his court had "jurisdiction of the parties and the subject matter," the judge concluded, "[it had] no jurisdiction to grant [said] mandamus." Unable to provide the desired remedy, Kennerly was forced, as he put it, to dismiss the case.

Similar suits — and outcomes — arose in cities across the state. Cases would be brought before Texas state and federal district courts only to have judges refuse to order injunctions, usually citing a number of procedural and, occasionally, substantive reasons for this opinion. In 1932, for instance, Judge Kennerly refused to rehear White's case, citing the past justifications for inaction and the technicality that the plaintiff's attorneys had given the defendants insufficient notice of the case. Kennerly also turned down a similar request from C. A. Booker of San Antonio for an injunction to allow blacks entrance into the Bexar County Democratic primary. Interestingly, in a later case filed in the state courts, State District Judge S. G. Taylor would grant Booker his injunction, but an immediate appeal delayed enforcement of the ruling until the election was over. Once the next election rolled around, a later ruling by the Texas Fourth Circuit Court of Appeals overturning Judge Taylor's injunction denied Booker and other San Antonio blacks access to the primary yet again. That same year, Judge Randolph Bryant of the U.S. District Court for the Northern District of Texas dismissed without prejudice a suit brought by Robert Williams of Grayson County and held under advisement a Jefferson County action filed by C. S. Eugene challenging the AWP. In neither case did the plaintiffs get to vote as they wished. In 1933, Julius White sued the Houston Democratic Party, seeking to vote in a primary election for city officials, only to have Judge Kennerly once again deny his plea on the grounds that, in barring blacks from voting, city Democrats had been acting under an "inherent power of the party." As city primaries involved no state power, Kennerly asserted, their conduct was not governed by *Nixon v. Herndon* or even by his opinion in *White v. Lubbock*. The year 1934, in turn, saw the Texas Supreme Court rule in the case of *Bell v. Hill*: "We are clearly of the opinion that the resolution passed by the Democratic State Convention at Houston was a valid resolution under the power clearly guaranteed to that body by the Bill of Rights of this State; and that since the action of that convention has never been revoked by another Democratic Convention, it is still the policy of the Democratic Party of this State, and that there exists no authority to permit negroes to vote in the Democratic primary of the State." And so the pattern of technical delays and outright refusals to act continued unchecked.

Then, in 1935, disaster struck the campaign against the AWP. Against the suggestion of the NAACP's lawyers (who warned that the Supreme Court's increasing conservatism boded ill for a voting-rights suit at that time), Wesley and Atkins brought another AWP case before the Supreme Court. As they perceived the situation, without the power of the vote, Texas blacks would be forever trapped in "poverty and self-hate." The AWP had to go. Moreover, the ongoing inability of Texas blacks to vote demonstrated that the NAACP's white lawyers could not appreciate how imperative it was to end the AWP in the fight against the inequities of segregation and discrimination. It was time for the fight to rest fully in the hands of the black community itself.

Wesley and Atkins's client was a charismatic and politically active Houston barber by the name of Richard Randolph Grovey. Collectively, Grovey, Wesley, and Atkins were (as the historian Darlene Clark Hine put it) "as determined to create a politically unified black community as they were committed to overthrowing the white primary." In fact, each saw the latter result as the best way to achieve the former goal. To this end, and drawing on years of political organization and agitation among the state's black communities, they brought suit in a Houston justice-of-the-peace court against the election judge Albert Townsend seeking damages of ten dollars. Since Texas law allowed appeals only of matters with damages valued at twenty dollars or more, this strategy permitted Grovey to appeal his subsequent loss directly to the U.S. Supreme Court. In early 1935, the Court agreed to hear the case and put the matter on its docket for argument. *Argument* turned out to be a relative term in this matter. Neither Texas nor the Democratic Party chose to argue the case. When, in March 1935, the Court undertook to decide the case, the justices had before them only the briefs provided by Grovey and his attorneys and the record of their submissions in oral argument. Despite the advantage that such a one-sided debate should have provided, the result in *Grovey v. Townsend* was a devastating loss for the AWP's opponents.

Once again, Wesley and Atkins failed to provide the justices with a narrowly focused argument, instead submitting a broad-based — even scattershot — list of arguments attacking the AWP. The Texas AWP was state action, they contended, because of the state's extensive regulation of the primary process. To prove this, they listed fifteen similarities between the state's regulation of the general elections and the Democratic primary. The AWP was also unconstitutional, they contended, because of its unequal treatment of African Americans in violation of the Fourteenth Amendment's equal protection clauses. And, even if the Democratic Party were held to be a private agency, given that the *national* Democratic Party had never authorized the AWP, the ban on black voting was still illegitimate. While all these were perfectly valid arguments, they lacked the unity of focus that the NAACP's lawyers had come to see as essential. The result, once again, was to provide the justices with the chance to pick and choose which arguments for or against the AWP they would base their judgment on — simply ignoring those whose dictates or implications forced them to act faster or go further than they wished.

The outcome of *Grovey v. Townsend* was much the same as that of *Nixon v. Condon* — only made worse by the Court's greater conservatism. Writing for a unanimous court, Justice Owen Roberts refused to accept Grovey's argument that Texas's primary elections were by their nature state action because of the state's extensive regulation. Texas's primary elections, Roberts explained, were not state action. Selectively choosing from Wesley and Atkins's brief only those examples that best suited his exclusionary intent, Justice Roberts noted that Texas did not pay for the primaries, furnish the ballots, or count the votes. How could the primaries be state action when the state failed to control these fundamental functions of an election? More to the point, given that the Texas Supreme Court had determined in *Bell v. Hill* (1934) — "a case definitely involving the point" — that the legislature of Texas had not "essayed to interfere, and indeed may not interfere, with the constitutional liberty of citizens to organize a party and to determine the qualifications of its members," how could the Court hold such primaries to be state action? "In the light of the principles so announced," Justice Roberts concluded, "we are unable to characterize the managers of the primary election as state officers in such sense that any action taken by them in obedience to the mandate of the state convention respecting eligibility to participate in the organization's deliberations, is state action." Political parties were private voluntary associations; by logical association, their primary elections were private matters also. The AWP was constitutional.

With these few words, fifteen years of attack on the AWP came to a screeching halt. Although, in 1938, Wesley and Atkins tried again to defeat the AWP in a suit filed before the U.S. District Court for the Southern District of Texas, the result was a foregone and disappointing conclusion. Defeat for the AWP seemed as far away as ever.

# CHAPTER 4

# Last Chance for Victory

*Smith v. Allwright* in

the Lower Federal Courts

At the time, the event that would develop into the case of *Smith v. Allwright* did not seem especially important. For years, registered black voters had presented themselves to vote in the Democratic primaries of Texas, and, for years, they had been turned away. It was expected. It was anticipated. It was actually, on a strategic level, the desired result. The idea was to keep the pressure on Texas Democrats and, in so doing, to build up a laundry list of vote denial so long and excessive that the courts would finally *have* to listen and move to end the all-white primary (AWP) once and for all.

As an officer in the Houston branch of the National Association for the Advancement of Colored People (NAACP), Dr. Lonnie Smith was merely doing his part when, on July 27, 1940, and again on August 24, he presented himself at the Forty-eighth Precinct of Harris County, Texas, to vote as a Democrat in the primary election. Denied access to the polls on account of his race by Precinct Judges S. E. Allwright and James J. Liuzza, Smith probably did not expect anything of substance to come of the matter — although he hoped that something would. In fact, Smith's attempt to vote was part of the NAACP's ongoing search for a plaintiff to challenge the AWP. However, experience taught the need for diminished expectations.

Symbolic efforts such as Dr. Smith's attempt to vote were a central part of the NAACP's strategy to defeat the AWP in the late 1930s. The 1935 defeat in *Grovey v. Townsend* had been a major setback for the AWP's opponents. (The Houston *Informer* actually compared it to the infamous Supreme Court case of *Dred Scott v. Sanford*, which had in 1857 struck down any federal attempts to restrict the expansion of slavery.) With a few short paragraphs, Justice Roberts negated over ten years of incremental victories when he declared the Texas Democratic Party a private voluntary association — and, thus, beyond the scope of the Fourteenth and Fifteenth Amendments. As the Court saw things, Texas did not pay for the primaries, furnish the ballots, or count the votes. As such, the primaries remained solely the private concern of the Texas Democratic Party. And, if that organization wanted to exclude someone from its nominating process, it was free to do so.

Using the courts as an instrument of social and political change had proved a much more difficult process than anticipated; the judges kept refusing to assume their intended role as avenging reformers, and, with *Grovey*, they had become active defenders of the AWP. All too aware of these sad facts, the AWP's opponents took an organizational and conceptual step back. They understood that an opportunity had been lost and, thus, that, for the time being, a frontal attack on the AWP was impossible.

Leaving aside the issue of fault (each side in the NAACP/Wesley-Atkins debate largely blamed the other for the defeat represented by *Grovey*), the lesson that *Grovey* taught was the urgent need for unity of effort *and* argument in the fight against the AWP. Defeats such as *Grovey* were an inevitable result when the AWP's opponents split their efforts. If the AWP were to be defeated in the future — and the NAACP never wavered in its commitment to that goal — it was imperative to turn inward. The highest priorities that the NAACP faced were to commence the slow process of strengthening organizational unity, to build up stronger local and national bases of operations, and, most important of all, to decide on a uniform litigation strategy for future attacks on the AWP.

In the five years following *Grovey*, this is exactly what happened. On the national level, the NAACP's leaders embraced three important truths about the enfranchisement campaign. First, they recognized that, for a litigation-based approach to civil rights reform to work, both dependable legal expertise and consistent legal argument were essential — they were, in fact, intimately related to each other. In practical terms, this recognition meant creating a full-time, in-house legal staff to exercise uniform, centralized control of the campaign against segregation and the AWP. Over time, this commitment to organizational unity resulted in the creation of a separate, fully staffed litigation arm for the association — first by reorganizing its National Legal Committee (NLC), but, ultimately, by creating an independent legal wing, the Legal Defense and Education Fund (LDF), established in March 1940. The LDF ultimately brought and argued the *Smith* case in the Supreme Court.

Legal consistency also meant being more proactive in selecting, organizing, and arguing the NAACP's case against the AWP. Before 1935, the national NAACP had never initiated an AWP case. Others challenged the AWP and brought suit in the courts. It was only then that the NAACP's lawyers took over the case, reacting to events rather than shaping them. Entering the case so late, however, often tied the NLC's hands. By the time a case was filed with a trial court, usually the basic facts and issues were already well established and, in fact, could not be disputed under the rules of appellate pleading. (Appellate courts decide matters of law only. Once a trial court has determined the facts in a case, all later arguments are made in the light of those factual determinations alone.) As a result, potentially winning arguments and legal strategies often could not be made because the originating lawyers had failed to set up the case properly. Worse yet, as *Grovey* had shown, without careful preparation, dangerous legal and constitutional defects could creep into such improperly prepared cases, defects that later exploded the NLC lawyers' best efforts in those and future cases. Letting the local branches bring large numbers of hastily prepared suits — or, worse, having a case brought independently of the NAACP, as with *Grovey* — was a path to failure. Far better for the NLC's lawyers to "guide" a case "from its very inception." Only then, as NAACP Executive Secretary Walter White noted in a 1940 memorandum, could they ensure that it was "being properly handled."

Implicit in these insights, and the basis of the second truth learned by the NAACP's national lawyers, was an admission that the NAACP had mishandled relations with the local branches, the wider communities that they served, and, hence, the litigation process as a whole. Grassroots support was essential if the campaign against the AWP were to succeed. Unfortunately, as the events surrounding *Grovey* showed, relations between the NAACP and local community leaders in Texas were badly strained. At times, arguments between the two camps over issues of pacing and strategy — splits induced in large part by their differing perspectives as repeat players (RPs) and one shotters (OSs) — broke out into open warfare.

NAACP lawyers, for instance, were brutal in their condemnation of Atkins and Wesley's handling of *Grovey*. In El Paso, Fred Knollenberg complained to NAACP officials that Grovey's lawyers "had succeeded only in wasting . . . a considerable sum of money." James Marshall of the NLC described the case in correspondence as "badly mishandled": "The points that we intended to raise were either omitted or not presented in clear form." Another longtime NAACP lawyer sarcastically described the two breakaway lawyers as "our baby lawyers at Houston." Had they been in charge of this case, each implied, things would have been different. As NAACP Director of Branches William Pickens explained in a 1935 letter: "This decision might possibly have been to the contrary if the briefs had been drawn by more experienced constitutional lawyers [meaning the NAACP's lawyers] and if the matter had been presented in a different light to the court."

On the other side, Atkins, Wesley, and their supporters in Texas attacked the national office as elitist and even racist. Their decision to bring *Grovey* on their own had been mostly rooted in their distrust of the NLC lawyers — a distrust that crystallized largely in reaction to that office's arrogance and racial imbalance. No longer were Texas blacks willing to accept directives from above quietly; they expected, and needed, to have their opinions asked and skills used. In May 1935, Jack Atkins explained his reasons for independent action in a letter to Charles Hamilton Houston. Arguing that the NAACP ignored the work of black lawyers in the fight against the AWP, he noted how R. D. Evans of Waco had been one of the first lawyers to bring a primary case to court — yet, "when the N.A.A.C.P. came to file its first Nixon case, it ignored Evans, ignored the lay leadership in *Love v. Griffith*, paid its money to white lawyers and went on its merry way." Atkins found this situation unacceptable. The fight for black civil rights *had* to rest in the hands of the black community itself, and, at least as far as the NAACP's national efforts were concerned, it did not. Atkins thus ended his letter with the warning that, without his and other Texas blacks' support, the NAACP was doomed to be "practically a non-entity in Texas."

By 1935, NAACP leaders were beginning to see Atkins's point. Although they rejected the idea that only members of a particular group could advocate effectively for that group as racist and factually inaccurate, the perception that they were somehow insensitive toward the legitimate concerns of local black communities — not to mention that they were ignoring the legal talent found in those communities on account of race — was another matter. The Texans were not the only ones to challenge the national office's leadership in civil rights matters. Local branches across the South were making similar complaints about management styles, litigation strategies, and the pacing of reform. Clearly, the situation in Texas was not simply the case of power-hungry locals and clashing personalities. These and similar splits between the home office and the local branches would have to be rectified if a campaign against the AWP were to succeed. The NAACP now understood this fact. The question was how to achieve this unity.

Finally, and largely as a response to complaints from the local branches and other black community leaders, the NAACP accepted that its reorganized legal team needed to have black members — and that, ideally, it should be headed by a skilled African American lawyer. Some questions remained as to how many blacks to appoint to the NLC. Walter White, for instance, was cautious about just how many blacks to include; although he saw the advantages of "add[ing] so many colored lawyers," he feared that this step would ignore skilled white attorneys who could also help the NAACP achieve victory. Still, on the basic point of including black lawyers, consensus reigned supreme. With an ever-rising number of skilled young black lawyers coming out of such law schools as Howard University and expressing an interest in taking on the fight for equal rights, there were very good reasons to include them and no good reasons not to. By 1936, an expanded advisory legal committee included large numbers of young, energetic, and committed African American lawyers.

The acknowledgment of these three truths by the NAACP's leadership redefined the NAACP's fight against the AWP. In fact, the need for greater centralized control over the litigation process necessitated a broadening of the membership — and leadership — of the campaign against the AWP. Without increased centralized control, legal victory was largely unattainable, yet, without greater accountability to, and understanding within, the black community, centralized control was a resource beyond the NLC's grasp. Control through unity was the new watchword, and most of the NAACP's organizational activities throughout the last half of the 1930s sought this end.

The achievement of this revised organizational objective started with the hiring of one man: Charles Hamilton Houston. Not long after the debacle of *Grovey,* the association turned to Houston, an African American lawyer and vice dean of Howard University Law School, to serve as special counsel and head of the newly reorganized NLC. Houston proved a brilliant choice. As a first lieutenant in the army during the First World War, Houston had experienced racism firsthand and returned from the war convinced, as he later wrote, that "I would study law and use my time fighting for men who could not strike back." In 1918, Houston attended Harvard Law School, where he was the first African American to be asked to join that school's law review. Following graduation, Houston entered private practice with his father in Washington, D.C. He later joined the faculty of Howard University Law School as a part-time instructor. In 1929, Houston became the law school's vice dean and began a multiyear campaign to enhance its effectiveness and reputation as a training ground for African American lawyers, stressing always that "a lawyer's either a social engineer or he's a parasite on society." By the early 1930s, Houston was working with the NAACP on a part-time basis, bringing with him many of his most talented students from Howard. In 1935, he took a leave of absence from Howard and joined the NAACP full-time as special counsel. One year later, he named his former student, Thurgood Marshall, as his assistant (and eventual successor).

On taking office, Houston set out to improve relations with the local branches and the wider black community. As early as 1934, he had noted in a memorandum to the NAACP leadership that the principal objective behind legal campaigns such as that attacking the AWP should be "to arouse and strengthen the will of local communities to demand and fight for their rights." To this end, he argued: "A great deal of travel and personal contact work will have to be done in order to insure that the cases are being carefully and vigorously handled, and that the local people are not frightened off." The NAACP, Houston contended, needed "as many tie-ins with other organizations as possible." Without such ties and the commitment to united action that they implied, Houston noted, victory was doubtful.

What Houston understood, and soon convinced the NAACP's officers to accept, was that, without coordinated action, a local community's enthusiasm for change often led it to undertake imprudent or mistimed actions (such as filing a primary case alone) beyond its ability to achieve. Alternately, defeats such as *Grovey* could, and did, discourage local members frustrated by their continued inability to vote. As Houston explained in a November 1935 memorandum: "This means that we have to stop or at least slow down until we have developed a sustaining mass interest behind the program. . . . The social and public factors must be developed at least along with and, if possible, before the actual litigation commences." With contact, then, came the ability both to encourage ongoing resistance to the AWP and to head off incautious responses — and, with each, the concurrent ability to shape the litigation process.

Houston's blueprint for creating coordinated action between the national office and the branches began by building closer ties between the NAACP and the growing numbers of skilled black lawyers spread out across the South. Houston understood the leadership role that the black bar played in the South. Over the preceding ten years, the number of skilled Southern black lawyers had expanded rapidly. Most had studied at Howard and other black law schools and had been trained in the gospel of law as "social engineering." Increasingly, these young lawyers were taking the lead in the fight against segregation and other legal discriminations. Or, perhaps more accurately, they were willing to take on the task of leadership — if asked. Houston stressed this last point when he proposed increasing the number of black lawyers on the NLC. Responding to Walter White's fear of alienating white lawyers by appointing too many blacks to the committee, Houston responded: "I agree about some good white lawyers, but what I want to do is get the local works strengthened in the field."

Young, energetic, and "willing to travel around and undergo the inconveniences and hardships, tensions and physical dangers involved in going to try cases in southern communities," these black lawyers were a legal and organizational resource that Houston was desperate to tap. As he noted in a September 1936 memorandum to Walter White and Arthur Springarn, it was imperative that the NAACP make use of all black lawyers "who have some contribution . . . to make," no matter how small.

Finding skilled black lawyers was only a beginning. Houston also understood that keeping control over the litigation processes demanded that he build closer ties to the local branches themselves — especially, with respect to the AWP, with the contentious local branches in Texas.

{ *The Battle for the Black Ballot* }

During the five years that he served as NAACP special counsel, Houston logged thousands of miles traveling to meet with members of these branches. His message was a combination of strategic caution matched with an "evangelistic" call for unified action and institutional support for organization building. (In fact, in a letter to Thurgood Marshall, Houston once described his role as being "not only lawyer but evangelist and stump speaker.") It proved an enticing message. Caught up in the vitality of Houston's message, Texas officials of the NAACP organized a membership drive in 1936. In October of that year, this drive culminated in the formation of the Texas State Conference of Branches of the NAACP. Now centrally organized, the Texas NAACP set out under the guidance of Houston and the NLC to raise the funds necessary to renew the campaign to defeat the AWP. Even Jack Atkins, long a critic of the NLC, was becoming "more and more convinced that the grave legal questions like this one need expert direction and leadership from Negro counsel occupying some such position as that which [Houston held] with the NAACP."

As Atkins's acceptance of centralized control of litigation shows, Houston was extremely successful in his organizational efforts as special counsel. Increasingly satisfied that they were no longer ignored by the national office — and realizing that, if they were to achieve the dream of widespread African American voting, they needed the NAACP just as much as the NAACP needed them — local branches throughout Texas came to accept Houston's leadership in the fight against the AWP. Problems still remained, of course. As OSs, Texas blacks were still more anxious to bring an immediate case than were the NAACP's RP lawyers in New York. Pleas to Houston to act now were common. And, although the Texans generally accepted Houston's explanation that the association was "a little short of cash," they still kept pushing for action. In 1938, impatient members of the Houston branch even brought another AWP suit on their own, *Richardson v. Executive Committee of the Democratic Party for the City of Houston*, which they argued — and lost — before Judge Kennerly of the U.S. District Court for the Southern District of Texas.

Still, as the decade came to a close, Houston's hard work meant that most of the players were now on the same page regarding the NAACP's leadership in the fight to end the AWP. Houston's next step was to find a workable strategy capable of defeating the AWP. Abandoning the fight against the AWP was never an option. Houston viewed *Grovey* as "pure legalism" and criticized Justice Roberts for not recognizing the "verities of the situation." As early as May 1935, the NAACP's in-house journal, *The Crisis*, argued: "While *Grovey v. Townsend* delivered a heavy blow at the Negro's status as a citizen in the South, it cannot long stand in the way of qualified Negroes securing the ballot." Still, *Grovey* placed a heavy burden on those seeking to end the AWP. Whether *Grovey* was historically doomed or not, how could Houston and his staff defeat the AWP when the law of the land considered political parties to be private associations?

In an effort to find an answer to this question — and as a means of improving ties with Texas lawyers and branch officials — Houston put out a call for help. On June 9, 1938, for instance, he asked Fred Knollenberg to research whether the state — in actual fact, if not under the letter of the law — paid the costs of Texas primary elections. His hope was that, if he could show how Texas actually covered the costs of the Democratic primary, he could undermine *Grovey*'s holding that the primary was simply the private concern of a private organization. As Knollenberg sadly noted in his response, although state law outlined every other step in the primary process, "the only thing they did not do was provide for the payment of the costs," which was "placed upon the candidates." In a series of memorandums, Houston also asked the state branches to "compile a very factual examination of the operation of the primary that would disclose a comprehensive state control and supervision." He hoped that, with the facts provided by this analysis, he could make the justices "look through the subterfuge of private party regulation and declare that in essence the primary is a public-state-controlled undertaking and therefore comes within the prohibitions of the Fourteenth and Fifteenth Amendments."

As the state branches collected their data in the two years that followed, Houston and Thurgood Marshall, Houston's successor as special counsel (Houston resigned from his post in early 1940 for reasons of ill health), continued to call for suggestions and data that would undermine the AWP's legal foundation. Carter Wesley, for example, carried out an extensive correspondence with Marshall and other NAACP officials, full of advice and suggestions. Other local leaders, such as Marceo Smith from Dallas, carried out smaller, but still substantial, dialogues as well.

Still, through the rest of the 1930s, Houston and Marshall continued to stress the need for caution and delay. Fearing that a premature action would fail, and all too aware that this was likely to be their last chance to defeat the AWP, Houston and Marshall were hesitant to act. Better to continue strengthening their arguments for when the time to act was ripe.

On the whole, the local branches accepted this logic and the resulting requests for delay. Except for the Houston branch's 1938 suit, Texas blacks waited for the word from the newly organized LDF that it was time to act; some waited impatiently, but they waited nonetheless. With the arrival of the 1940 election cycle, however, conditions began to seem more conducive to victory. With changes in the Supreme Court's makeup, new leadership on both the NAACP's Texas State Conference of Branches and its Houston branch office, and general NAACP membership growing across the state, most of the pieces for a renewed attack at last seemed to be in place. The only part still missing was a new legal justification for ending the AWP. Still, fearing that too much delay could be as costly as too little, Marshall decided that it was time to set into motion the long-awaited attack on the AWP.

At the annual meeting of the Texas State Conference of Branches in Corpus Christi in May 1940, Marshall laid out his plan of attack, including his demand for total control of the case from beginning to end. Already anxious to act, the conference members welcomed Marshall's proposals with open arms. In response to Marshall's suggestions, the conference determined that control over the case was, in fact, best left in the hands of Marshall and the LDF — although it suggested the appointment of a Texas lawyer to help coordinate the fight on the local level. (Ultimately, W. J. Durham, a skilled courtroom attorney from Sherman, Texas, accepted this post.) The Texas board also agreed to back a single case of Marshall's choice; after meeting with leading black Texas lawyers, Marshall decided that the case should be filed by the well-funded, aggressive Houston branch. To raise funds, the conference organized the statewide Democratic Primary Defense Fund and, at Marshall's urging, issued an open invitation to all black lawyers to join a statewide legal advisory committee.

Marshall's next step was to find a plaintiff to file his new case. Working with the Reverend Albert A. Lucas, recently elected president of the Houston branch, Marshall sought a "perfect" plaintiff. Whoever took on that role would have to be committed to the cause since, even at this late date, serving as plaintiff in a civil rights suit was dangerous. The candidate would also have to be a citizen of outstanding reputation. Marshall's whole case was based on the illogic and unfairness of excluding *qualified* voters from the one election that had meaning; a plaintiff with a shady past could quickly derail this argument in the judges' eyes. Finally, Marshall needed someone willing to follow his lead in setting up the case. Marshall understood the effect that a defeat would have on the campaign against the AWP—and that against segregation in general. This might possibly be his last chance to defeat the AWP. No detail was too small, no concern too minor. He had to get it right the first time.

After days of consultation, Marshall and Lucas finally settled on two possible candidates: Sidney Hasgett and Dr. Lonnie Smith. Each was an established member of Houston's black community. Hasgett was a hod carrier working in the construction trade. (A hod is a trough used to carry bricks and rivets for building.) Smith was a dentist. Each was well-known and respected for his personal character and commitment to change. And each was willing to serve as plaintiff. Perhaps most important of all, however, each was a known quantity found close at hand. (Not only were Smith and Hasgett the second and third vice-presidents of the Houston branch, respectively; each was also a member of Reverend Lucas's own congregation.) Using one of them as plaintiff was, thus, both logical and effortless.

In the end, the decision was to go with Hasgett—with Smith's case held in reserve, just in case. Accordingly, as the polls opened on July 27, both Hasgett and Smith dutifully walked to their local precincts and sought to vote in the Democratic primary. Each was then—just as dutifully—turned away by the precinct judges. One month later, in the August 24 runoff election, the outcome was the same: Hasgett, accompanied by Houston branch leaders Grovey, Wesley, and Julius Smith, among others, as witnesses, was once again denied the ballot. (So too was Smith, although with much less fanfare.) Hasgett was even directly challenged on this occasion by the election judge, who noted: "You haven't been coming up here for the past nine or ten years. Now speak up, who sent you here?" Wesley's response on Hasgett's behalf was "the black citizens of Houston," who deserved the right to vote.

Marshall had his case. What he did not have, unfortunately, was a new legal argument with which to attack the AWP. So long as *Grovey* was law — and it would remain valid law unless overturned by the courts — Marshall's only legal option was to repeat the often-made contention that the Democratic primary was *in fact* the real election in Texas and, as such, was covered by the Fourteenth and Fifteenth Amendments' requirements. Still, Marshall was optimistic that the statistical evidence collected by the branch offices in the preceding two years gave him the tools to demonstrate, as Carter Wesley wrote in a September 11 letter to Marshall, "that this Primary [was] merely subterfuge." Barring a doctrinal shift by the Supreme Court, it was all he had.

With all this on his mind, Marshall brought suit on Hasgett's behalf before Judge Kennerly of the U.S. District Court for the Southern District of Texas against Election Judges Theodore Werner and John H. Blackburn on January 14, 1941. Arguing before the court on April 24, Marshall contended that — notwithstanding *Grovey* — the Democratic Party primary *was* a creation of the State of Texas and that, as such, it was of necessity subject to public regulation under the Fifteenth Amendment.

As Marshall saw it, the act of voting consisted of three interrelated steps: (1) qualifying to vote; (2) picking candidates; and (3) voting in the election. Past rulings by the Supreme Court made clear the right of African Americans to participate free of state interference in steps 1 and 3 of this process. Logic alone demanded that step 2 must also be protected. More to the point, so did an examination of the statutes regulating primary elections.

Drawing on the evidence collected for him by the local branches, Marshall compared some fifteen different state laws regulating every aspect of both primary and general elections. In many cases, not only were the requirements of the primary and general election laws the same (with the sole exception of substituting the term *primary* for the term *general*), but the primary and general election laws were also found in the same statute. Article 2930 of the Texas Revised Statutes, for instance, required that election officials in both the general and the primary elections be qualified voters; Section 2955 imposed the exact same rules for disqualification irrespective of whether the election was deemed primary or general. In fact, with the exception of who paid the costs of holding the different elections — and, of course, the Democratic Party's rule banning black voting — the Democratic Party depended almost exclusively on state statutes to organize, regulate, and legitimize its primaries. This, Marshall contended, made the Democratic primary state action. Add that more Texans voted in the Democratic primary than in the general election — often in proportions double or even triple the number who voted in the general election — and the central and public nature of the primary election was unavoidable.

The defense lawyers countered these arguments by once again noting that primaries were *not* elections but merely mechanisms for choosing candidates to run in the "actual" (general) elections. Given that Hasgett was free to vote in the general election, they insisted, the Fifteenth Amendment's requirements were satisfied. They added the assertion that, as a private agency, the Democratic Party was free to set its membership rules as it pleased. Given that the state convention had chosen to limit membership to white Texans, Hasgett was not — and by definition could not be — a member of the party; hence, he was properly excluded from the July and August 1940 primaries. Given the Supreme Court's ruling in *Grovey*, the defense concluded, the point was settled, and a ruling in favor of the defendants was required.

Ruling on May 5, Judge Kennerly found himself in complete agreement with the defense. Despite Marshall's best efforts to convince him of the public nature of the Democratic primary, Kennerly felt bound by the Supreme Court's ruling in *Grovey* to uphold the Democratic Party's private status. That large numbers of Democrats chose — for some reason — to vote in the primary but not in the general election did nothing to change this fact. Barring a shift in Supreme Court doctrine, the Democratic state convention had the power to exclude black voters from its primary.

Because they had expected Kennerly's negative ruling, Marshall and his team of lawyers were prepared to appeal to the Fifth Circuit Court of Appeals in New Orleans. With the case set to be heard in November, they quickly began work on their appeal. Yet before the appeal could be argued — in fact, before they could do much of any work on the appeal — the Supreme Court handed down a decision that changed the entire context of the AWP dispute.

Announced on May 26, 1941, the Court's ruling in *United States v.*

*Classic* seemed to offer Marshall the unique opening to attack the AWP that he had been searching for. *Classic* was an appeal by the Justice Department challenging the dismissal by a judge in the U.S. District Court for the Eastern District of Louisiana of a criminal indictment charging voter fraud against a number of local commissioners of elections. As such, *Classic* did not directly pose the issues raised by the AWP (or, in fact, any issue involved with race). Rather, the case focused on charges that election officials in the Second Congressional District of Louisiana manipulated the vote in the September 10, 1939, Democratic primary election to defeat members of the dominant Long political machine. The government argued that, by denying eligible voters a genuine chance to choose the candidate of their choice, this fraud violated federal statutes making it a crime to deny anyone "any right or privilege . . . secured by the Constitution." The defendants, citing the Supreme Court precedent in *Newberry v. United States*, countered that Congress did not have the power to regulate primary elections and, thus, denied congressional authority to legislate in these matters. The district judge agreed and threw out the case.

Appealing directly to the Supreme Court on a writ of error, the government argued strongly that, "as a matter of law, the Louisiana primary elections determine the candidates at the general election." Further, the government lawyers noted how, "as a matter of unbroken practice, the Democratic primary election determines the victor at the general election." Given both these facts, to deny Congress the right to regulate the process by which federal offices were chosen was illogical. "If the machinery of choice involves two elections, primary and general, rather than one," they concluded, "the right to participate in the choice must include both steps."

Writing for a five-to-three majority (Chief Justice Hughes had been lead attorney in an earlier primary case, *Newberry v. United States*, and, thus, recused himself in *Classic*), Justice Harlan Fiske Stone adopted this logic. As he saw the case, Louisiana, "in common with many other states," had exercised its "discretion by setting up machinery for the effective choice of party candidates for representative in Congress by primary elections, and by its laws it [had] eliminate[d] or seriously restrict[ed] the candidacy at the general election of all those who [were] defeated at the primary." Such rules, Stone argued, made the Louisiana primary "an integral part" of the election process. Given

this fact, voter fraud in a primary election was by definition "an interference with the effective choice of the voters" — at least where one
could show "as a matter of fact and law" that the primary election
both served as "the only stage of the election procedure when [the
voters'] choice [was] of significance" and was "the only stage when
such interference could have any practical effect on the ultimate
result." When this could be shown, the Constitution's dictates were
clear. "We cannot close our eyes to the fact," Stone intoned for the
majority, "that the practical influence of the choice of candidates at
the primary may be so great as to affect profoundly the choice at the
general election, even though there is no effective legal prohibition
upon the rejection at the election of the choice made at the primary,
and may thus operate to deprive the voter of his constitutional right
of choice." Put another way, as long as the primary was "either by law
or in fact, influential upon the election," the Constitution guaranteed
a voter's "right to participate in the procedure of choice."

The implications of the *Classic* ruling for the AWP were obvious.
By integrating the concept of primaries into that of elections (at least
where primary elections were "an integral part" of the election process), the Court seemed to be effectively overturning its ruling in
*Grovey.* Yet had it? In actuality, the Court never mentioned *Grovey* in
its ruling. And, given the Court's stress on the "integral part" limita-
tion in its ruling, not to mention that *Classic* directly affected only primaries held for federal offices, *Classic* arguably did *not* affect the
constitutionality of the Texas AWP. Still, *Classic* provided Marshall
with a new means to circumvent the whole private association defense
of the AWP. The Court seemed to be saying in *Classic* that, where
state law made the primary an integral part of the election machinery
and the primary inevitably produced the winner at the general election, that election was regulated under federal law regardless of the
party's private or public status.

Of course, proving that the Texas Democratic primary was an integral part of the election process was not going to be easy. Still, reading Stone's opinion as proof of a doctrinal shift in the Court's views
about the nature and effect of voting in a primary election, Marshall
was optimistic that *Classic* for once put the Supreme Court on his side.
As the *Houston Informer* gleefully proclaimed: "Whereas the Democratic Party had had all the protection and Negroes have been forced

to scurry and hunt like beavers for a hole to get through, now the Negroes seemingly are sitting on top of the world, and the Democratic Party will have to burrow and hunt and dig to find a way to get by the famous Classic case."

Strategically, *Classic* meant abandoning the upcoming *Hasgett* appeal. Hasgett's case involved state offices only, not federal. In what now proved to be an oversight, Marshall had in his *Hasgett* complaint objected only to the August 24 runoff primary election. Unfortunately, the candidates for federal office were chosen during the July 27 primary and, thus, were not on that particular ballot. Given that *Classic* dealt only with federal offices (although Marshall himself argued that *Classic* extended to state offices as well as federal), this fact meant that the *Hasgett* appeal could not easily draw on *Classic* in making its case.

Concerned with issues of "strategy and timing," as he put it in a December 1941 letter, Marshall therefore proposed abandoning the *Hasgett* appeal and filing an entirely new case, one that did involve federal offices and, thus, could be "based upon the theory of the case of *United States v. Classic.*" This was not the most popular of decisions back in Texas. Julius White warned Marshall that he "had better win the next case or not return to Texas," and Marshall noted in a November 17, 1941, letter that, were he to lose this case, he would have to move to Germany and live with "Adolf Hitler or some other peace loving individual who would be less difficult than the Negroes in Texas who had put up money for the case." Nonetheless, the search for a new plaintiff began immediately. In the end, after toying with a case from Dallas, Marshall settled on his "reserve" plaintiff, Dr. Smith. As had Hasgett, Smith had attempted to vote in both the July 27 and the August 24 primary elections (he had even tried to obtain an absentee ballot before these dates), and, as his case had not yet been filed, it could now be structured to include the all-important federal element.

Filing his complaint before Judge Kennerly on November 13, 1941, Marshall made his strategy clear: he had to convince the court that the Democratic Party primary was, as currently organized, an integral part of the electoral process in Texas despite the party's supposed private nature. If he could do this, Marshall was confident that the logic of *Classic* demanded an end to the AWP. The question was whether he could do it.

Brought to trial in April 1942, Marshall's case looked remarkably like the one that he had just argued before the same court in *Hasgett*. In fact, given the similarities between the two cases, both sides not only consented to use the testimony and exhibits from the hearings and trial of the earlier case but also agreed to an extensive stipulation of the facts. All acknowledged that Smith had attempted to vote in the July and August 1940 primaries and had been turned away on account of his race; that the Democratic candidate in the general election almost always won; that the election in question had involved federal offices; and that much of the election machinery for the Democratic primary was organized and run by elected state and local officials. The defendants accepted that, except for his race, Smith was a qualified voter for the general election and "a believer in the tenets of the Democratic Party." And Marshall consented to a statement that the Democratic Party's resolution denying blacks the vote had never been annulled or repealed and that nothing in the operation of the Democratic primary as it currently existed deprived qualified Texas blacks from voting in the general election.

Ultimately, as Judge Kennerly noted in his judgment, *Smith* was effectively the same case as *Hasgett*; the only thing that had changed was the effect that *Classic* would, or would not, have on the outcome. Well aware of this fact, Marshall had in his complaint stressed the intrinsic and extensive nature of the Democratic primary in shaping Texas's electoral system. He argued not only that state statutes required the Democrats to hold a primary but also that the very operation of the primary was organized and regulated by state law. "Primary elections in Texas were created by statute and have been maintained solely by authority of the statutes of the State of Texas," Marshall declared. Nor, Marshall continued, did the Democratic Party exhibit the normal attributes of a private organization; it had no constitution, no membership rolls, not even any rules defining membership beyond excluding people of color and demanding that those joining the party consider themselves to be Democrats. Finally, given the statistics that he had already shown the court in *Hasgett* and filed once again in *Smith*, Marshall argued strongly that the court should accept the irrelevancy of the general election; with the Democratic candidate winning in all but a handful of elections since before the Civil War, the only election that mattered in Texas was the Democratic primary. In conclusion, Marshall stressed the similarities between this case and the situation in *Classic* and demanded an end to the AWP.

The defendants countered each argument point by point. Their formal answer to Smith's complaint denied Marshall's contention paragraph by paragraph, line by line. The Democratic Party was not a public entity. The defendants were not public officials but, rather, officers of the Democratic Party. Smith was denied access to the primary "solely because of the mandatory instructions of the Democratic Party," not as a result of any state law or dictate. In fact, the defendants especially denied "that the elections referred to in plaintiff's . . . petition [were] elections within the intent and meaning of Section 2 and 4 of Article 1 and Amendment Seventeen to the Constitution of the United States." At no time was Smith's right to vote limited by their actions. Nominees from the primaries, the defendants noted, had "no standing of any nature or kind in governmental affairs unless and until they are elected by all qualified voters in the general election," and nothing that either the defendants or their party had done was keeping Smith from this election. Notwithstanding the Supreme Court's ruling in *Classic, Grovey v. Townsend* was still the controlling doctrine here, and Smith's case should be thrown out.

Ruling on May 11, 1942, Judge Kennerly found once again for the defendants. As Kennerly saw matters, the only issue before the court was the impact of *Classic*. If not for *Classic*, he noted, "this case could and would be quickly disposed of by citing *Grovey v. Townsend*." *Classic*, in turn, was a specific ruling with limited reach outside its specific fact pattern. Ultimately, for *Classic* to apply, two legal conditions had to be met: (1) that the primary be "an integral part of the procedure of choice" and (2) that "the primary effectively controls the choice" of "elected representatives." And, as Kennerly perceived the facts to bear out, in neither case did these requirements apply to the Texas context. "In Louisiana," Kennerly noted, "the State Law . . . made the primary 'an integral part of the procedure of choice.' In Texas it has not." Nor was he convinced that "the Democratic Primary in Texas 'determines the choice of the elected representative.' " Yet, even if this were the case, he was "not convinced that the Supreme Court would have based the ruling in the *Classic* case solely upon the second point, nor [was he] convinced that the Supreme Court intended to over-rule

*Grovey.*" All this being so, Kennerly held that the *Grovey* precedent remained in force and, thus, ruled against Smith.

Undeterred by Kennerly's ruling (which, given his judgment in *Hasgett*, Marshall had expected), Marshall quickly filed an appeal with the Fifth Circuit Court of Appeals. Not that he expected to win there either. The dominant judge on the Fifth Circuit was the same Joseph Hutcheson who, as a district judge in the late 1920s, had ruled repeatedly in favor of the AWP. Still, if Marshall were to get his case before the Supreme Court, he had to go through the Fifth Circuit. And, besides, there was a chance that Hutcheson and the other circuit judges might see in *Classic* the doctrinal sea change that Marshall perceived.

Sadly, Marshall's negative prediction proved all too accurate. Arguing in November 1942 before a three-judge panel chaired by Hutcheson and including Judges Samuel Sibley and Edward R. Holmes, Marshall repeated his contentions about the public nature of the Democratic primary in Texas. The Democratic Party, Marshall explained in oral argument before the court, was a "loose-joined organization with no constitution or by-laws." It had neither permanent officers nor fixed rules for party governance and allowed any white person to join at his or her own, not the party's, discretion. In fact, Marshall observed, "the only resolution we've been able to find that they've ever passed . . . is this one against the Negro." The party did not even pay the costs of running the primaries (the contrary view of which had been one of the foundations behind the Supreme Court's *Grovey* ruling). For, although the state and local county governments in Texas were formally required to cover only a few incidental costs of running a primary, in practice they actually picked up most, if not all, of the tab (the rest of the cost falling to the candidates themselves). More to the point, given that "since 1895 all Democratic nominees, for U.S. Congress and governor, have been elected in Texas, with two exceptions," and that more people in Texas voted in the Democratic primary than in the general election, the Texas Democratic primary was, Marshall contended, integral to the shaping of the political process in Texas. As such, it demanded the same response to exclusion in Texas that the Supreme Court had provided for Louisiana in *Classic*.

Countering these arguments, the attorney Glen A. Perry of Houston ignored *Classic* as much as possible and, instead, stressed the many similarities between *Grovey* and the case at hand. Reviewing the almost twenty-year history of litigation over the AWP, Perry argued that, inasmuch as the Democratic primary "was not an election within the intent and meaning" of the Constitution, what mattered in determining the proper judgment for this case was the status of the political party imposing the exclusion. If the party were public, then the law *might* have some claim on determining membership requirements. But this was not the case in Texas. "The decisions of the Supreme Court of the United States," Perry argued, made clear that "a political party is a private organization that has the right to prescribe qualifications for membership therein." And, this being the case, *Grovey* had settled the matter. "In a general way, every proposition advanced by the appellants in the case at bar was advanced in *Grovey v. Townsend*," Perry concluded — advanced and rejected. Judge Kennerly's ruling was proper and should be upheld.

Although this latter position emphasizing *Grovey* over *Classic* was logically the weaker of the two arguments made by the defendants, the appellate judges were drawn to it. Early in the proceedings, it became apparent that the judges were not sympathetic to Marshall's contentions on behalf of Smith. At one point during oral argument, Judge Hutcheson even exclaimed with seeming unease: "If everybody can vote in the Democratic primary, they would probably have to abolish the primary." By the time the judges issued their ruling, the outcome was clear. "The Texas statutes regulating party primaries which were considered in *Grovey v. Townsend* are still in force," Judge Hutcheson for the Court noted. In that decision: "They [the statutes] were held not to render the primary an election in the constitutional sense. There is no substantial difference between that case and this." And, while it was true, as the plaintiffs below argued, "that different principles were announced by the Supreme Court in *United States v. Classic*," there were "many points" on which *Smith* "differ[ed]" from *Classic*. As such, *Classic* did not apply to the Texas context. "The opinion of the court in [*Classic*]," Hutcheson noted, "did not overrule or even mention *Grovey v. Townsend*." This being the case, he concluded, "we may not overrule it" ourselves.

With only one court left in which to argue his case, Marshall and the LDF staff began work on a petition to the Supreme Court to review the *Smith* case. Although the goal all along had been to get to the Supreme Court — it was here that Marshall felt he had the best chance of victory—the move was still a momentous one. Everyone involved in the fight against the AWP felt that this was their last chance for victory. Fail in the Supreme Court, and the fight against the AWP was effectively over—and with it, perhaps, the growing momentum in the fight against segregation in general. The final act in the fight against the AWP was about to begin.

# CHAPTER 5

# May It Please the Court

## *Smith v. Allwright* in the Supreme Court

Argument before the Supreme Court is not easy. Along with the inevitable nerves that come from arguing before the highest court in the land, there is the real problem of figuring out how to convince at least five justices that your position is the right one. As Justice Sandra Day O'Connor noted to a PBS interviewer in 1988, the Supreme Court "does not take the easy cases." And difficult cases make for hard arguments. Even where the legitimacy of your cause seems obvious to you, it may not seem so to the justices. Worse yet, you cannot always depend on such familiar supports as precedent when arguing before the High Court. Unlike other courts, the Supreme Court has the power to ignore precedent and reverse even long-standing legal doctrine. The justices' job is to interpret the Constitution's meaning *in practice*, and, where they feel that past practices are wrong, they are duty bound to act. Then again, like most judges, Supreme Court justices do not *like* to overturn precedent. Given a choice, they will almost always leave existing precedents, existing landmarks of legal and constitutional interpretation, intact.

With *Smith v. Allwright*, these difficulties were especially prominent. Smith's lawyer, Thurgood Marshall, was arguing only his second case before the Court as National Association for the Advancement of Colored People (NAACP) special counsel. And, although he had the institutional support provided by twenty years of litigation against the all-white primary (AWP) to draw on, it was still up to him to construct an argument that would win—and win in a manner that Texas Democrats could not once again evade. Adding to Marshall's difficulties was the Court's ruling, just eight years earlier, in *Grovey v. Townsend*. To win, Marshall had somehow to convince the justices that recent events had undermined this precedent. Marshall hoped to use the Court's 1941 ruling in *United States v. Classic* as a lever to achieve this end, but, given that the Court had clearly written the *Classic* ruling *not* to engage the question of AWPs, its willingness to accept such arguments was open to doubt.

To Smith and Marshall's advantage, however, were recent changes in the makeup of the Supreme Court. Only two justices, Chief Justice Harlan Fiske Stone and Justice Owen Roberts, remained from the Court that had ruled in *Grovey*. The new justices, in turn, had all been named by Democratic President Franklin D. Roosevelt. Most shared Roosevelt's liberal views of questions of government power, federalism, and individual rights. Even the Court's one member from the Deep South, Hugo L. Black of Alabama, was a passionate defender of individual rights — and many in the civil rights community saw him as being at least open-minded on the issue of race-based civil rights.

Moreover, while the Court's unwillingness to use its *Classic* ruling to tackle the AWP was annoying, it was not an insuperable roadblock. Highly aware of the powers intrinsic to their judicial function, the justices often limit the reach of their rulings to *just* the issues brought before them by the case at hand. They thus leave the wider implications of a ruling — such as *Classic*'s impact on the AWP — to future cases. This institutional mind-set meant that the justices' views on the AWP might not be set in stone. Still, convincing even new justices to abandon a clear precedent — especially one just eight years old — would be a difficult task.

Such was Marshall's burden as he set out to argue the *Smith* case in the summer and fall of 1943. Arguing a major constitutional case before the Court is an extended process. It actually begins with the original motions and arguments before the trial court. A good lawyer always plans ahead and lays a foundation within his original arguments for possible appeals. With a case such as *Smith*, where the goal all along was to get to the Supreme Court, laying the groundwork was imperative. To this end, Marshall had made sure that he and his colleagues took adequate care to frame the original case presented to Judge Kennerly. He knew that the appellate judges would get the case's entire record of proceedings — including Judge Kennerly's statement of his reasoning in his opinion ruling against them. A misstated argument here, an ignored issue there, might plant the seeds of doubt in the justices' minds — seeds that might later bear painful fruit as the arguing process within the Supreme Court progressed.

More to the point, proceedings in the trial and lower appellate courts would define the constitutional issues and arguments that the parties would eventually present to the Supreme Court. By the time Marshall found himself standing before the nine justices, he *knew* which issues he needed to stress and which issues he needed to avoid at all costs. And, whereas the Supreme Court's greater openness to considering the policy implications of disputes over constitutional law meant that new arguments were possible, the same arguments that had lost at the lower level would win or lose the case here.

Before he could argue before the justices, however, Marshall first had to get them to accept Smith's case for review. Unlike the circuit courts, which must hear every case coming from the district courts, the Supreme Court chooses which cases it hears. In this period, the Court's cases fell into two categories. The smaller category was that of appeals as of right — appellants in only a few small categories of cases could have the right to have the justices hear their appeals. Most cases, including *Smith*, fell into a different category, discretionary appeals. Those bringing such cases were required by the justices to file a special kind of brief, called *a petition for a writ of certiorari*. If the justices voted to accept that petition, the Court sent a judicial order, or writ, to the lower court; this writ of certiorari said: "Send us the full record of this case; we want to reexamine it." If the Court rejected the petition, the lower court's ruling and reasoning stood undisturbed. Refusing a petition for a writ of certiorari did not mean that the justices accepted the merits of the lower court's decision — only that they saw no reason to reexamine it. Even so, because Judge Kennerly in the district court and Judge Hutcheson on the Fifth Circuit both had ruled in favor of the AWP and both had rejected challenges to its constitutionality, refusing Marshall's petition for a writ of certiorari would have ended the campaign against the AWP.

Those filing a petition for a writ of certiorari (then as now) need the votes of at least four justices for the Court to accept their case for review. Although it might seem easy to satisfy what Court watchers call the "Rule of Four," getting four justices to vote to take a case was (and still is) often difficult. The justices have only a finite period of time in which to do their work. They therefore protect their dockets vigorously. Generally, the justices will accept a case only when they believe that the constitutional issues raised are both important and unsettled. In fact, of the thousands of certiorari petitions filed with the Court every year, at most two hundred are normally accepted.

The justices sift the piles of certiorari petitions and make their final decisions to grant or reject them in a conference in which they alone participate — in fact, one in which they are the only people in the room. Given the private nature of these proceedings, it is unclear how many justices voted to grant Smith's certiorari petition. However, on the basis of comments made in the subsequent trial conference (the meeting in which the justices decide the outcome of the case on the merits and for which we have notes from at least one of the justices), we can say that at least five justices felt that the questions raised by *Smith* were both important and, given the Court's ruling in *Classic*, in need of adjudication. In any case, the Court granted certiorari in *Smith v. Allwright* on June 7, 1943, and set it for argument on November 12, 1943.

Marshall thus had five months to organize his resources for one last push. His first step in preparing his case was to seek outside help. The greater the forces arrayed against the AWP, the better the chances of defeating it — or so he hoped. Happily, Marshall and the NAACP had their supporters. Within weeks, the American Civil Liberties Union, the National Lawyers Guild, and the Workers Defense League filed amicus briefs on Smith's behalf. Each mirrored the arguments that Marshall was ultimately to make before the Court. The ally that Marshall wanted most, however, was the federal government. *Classic*, after all, had been a government case brought by the U.S. Justice Department. Given the government's arguments in *Classic* in favor of an expansive definition of the right to vote, Marshall hoped that the Justice Department's lawyers would take a similar stance in *Smith*.

Unfortunately for Smith and Marshall, such support was not forthcoming. Although some in the Justice Department sympathized with the NAACP's position, most of the department's leadership refused to act. Their reasons varied. Herbert Wechsler, the lead government attorney in *Classic*, saw flaws in Marshall's attempt to extend the *Classic* ruling to the Texas situation. Reading *Classic* narrowly, Wechsler thought that it had not dealt with the issues at the heart of *Smith* — the power of a political party to select and limit its own membership. *Classic*, after all, had dealt with the effects of an electoral fraud that undermined the primary vote of those *already within* the party. At issue in

*Smith* were rules imposed by the party excluding otherwise qualified voters from the primaries. More to the point, Wechsler also feared the political fallout of Justice Department support — in particular, the negative reaction of the conservative, Southern-dominated Senate Judiciary Committee.

Ultimately, this last concern motivated Justice Department inaction. Solicitor General Charles Fahy, for instance, wrote to Attorney General Francis Biddle, warning: "Although the legal questions have difficulties, whether or not to participate is essentially a policy question. We have already assisted the Negroes by winning the Classic case which gives them their principal ammunition. Should we go further in their behalf and make a gesture which cannot fail to offend many others, in Texas and the South generally, in a case in which we are not a party? I think not." Biddle was equally blunt in his policy-based analysis for President Roosevelt: "If we intervened here again, the South would not understand why we were continually taking sides." (Biddle's and Roosevelt's concerns arose, not only because the Southern congressional leadership belonged to the president's party, but also because most Southern whites voted Democratic. Given the white South's racial views, any visible support of black voting rights would cause major political problems for the president.)

On a more positive note, in 1943, Fred Folsom, a Justice Department staff attorney, wrote an article for the *Columbia Law Review* supporting Marshall's contentions. In particular, Folsom argued that *Classic*'s incorporation of primaries into the electoral process — "where primary election laws operate to restrict seriously the choice of candidates at the general election" — had modified the context within which *Grovey* had been decided. In Folsom's view, Texas, like Louisiana, used a dual-phase electoral system in which the primary constrained the eventual outcome of the general election. And, given the Court's ruling in *Classic*, this constraint brought the Texas Democratic Party primary within the reach of the Fourteenth and Fifteenth Amendments.

Still, except for Folsom's unofficial analysis of *Classic*'s impact, Marshall was on his own as far as the federal government was concerned. Undeterred, Marshall, William H. Hastie (then dean of Howard Law School), the Legal Defense and Education Fund (LDF) legal staff, and the Texas attorney W. J. Durham set to work on Smith's Supreme

Court brief during August 1943. Marshall and his colleagues knew that they had a lot of work to do and not a whole lot of time in which to do it.

Fortunately, part of their job was already completed. In his certiorari petition, Marshall had already laid out the reasons why the Court should take the case. Starting with the contention that the Texas AWP denied nearly half a million African American citizens their constitutional right to a meaningful franchise, Marshall had made three broad arguments in favor of review in Smith's certiorari petition.

The first was that the Fifth Circuit had erred in its reading of *United States v. Classic. Classic*, Marshall argued, held that "where the state law has made the primary an integral part of the procedure of choice, or where in fact the primary effectively controls the choice, the right of the elector to have his ballot counted in the primary [is protected under federal law]." In its ruling, however, the Fifth Circuit had ignored one clear fact—in Texas, as in Louisiana, "the primary was 'an integral part of the procedure of choice.'" By ignoring this legally significant fact, the circuit court effectively denied Smith and others similarly situated the full reach of the Supreme Court's *Classic* ruling. This error needed correcting by the Court, the one institution that could do so.

Next, Marshall challenged the logic of the Court's 1935 ruling in *Grovey v. Townsend* in the light of the factual record provided in *Smith* and not available when the Court reached its decision in *Grovey*. As Marshall insisted, for the Court to allow the "practical disenfranchisement of . . . 11.86% of the total adult population . . . of Texas" to rest on such "inadequate" information was simply wrong and, thus, also demanded correction.

Finally, Marshall stressed the many inconsistencies between *Grovey* and *Classic*—inconsistencies that needed resolving. In fact, Marshall argued, had "the *Grovey* doctrine been applied in the *Classic* case it would have led to the conclusion that the election frauds were not 'under color of state law' because they were not authorized by the state." Clearly, such a confusion of interpretation needed resolving—"in accordance with the sound theory in the *Classic* case."

To these arguments, Marshall and his team of lawyers had to add specific reasons for the justices to act on the merits of the case and, hence, strike down the AWP. Which further arguments to include became a matter of heated debate. The LDF staff attorney Milton Konvitz argued that the case should be built on an aggressive application of the *Classic* ruling, advancing the idea that the primary was "an integral part of the procedure of choice as a matter of fact, regardless of the statutory situation." William Hastie pushed for a more limited reading of *Classic;* as he saw it, *Classic* had essentially overruled *Grovey,* and this reading of *Classic* could be a sound basis on which to construct the case. From Texas, Carter Wesley (speaking for himself and Jack Atkins) pressed for a "frontal attack" on *Grovey:* "I think as strong a case as possible should be made under the law of the *Classic* Case, then I think this *Grovey v. Townsend* Case should be faced straight-out and in the ultimate the facts in the *Grovey* Case, amplified and buttressed by the evidence of the Smith Case, should be used as the strongest factual basis for approaching the question raised in the current case." Marshall himself raised the possibility of attacking the AWP by undermining its state-law foundations; in a July 24, 1943, memorandum to the membership of the NAACP's National Legal Committee, Marshall introduced the idea that the brief should attack the "extent to which the Supreme Court . . . should be bound by state decisions on local issues," in particular, the "prior decision of the Texas Court in *Bell v. Hill* . . . as to the nature of political parties and primary elections in Texas."

Completed by early September 1943, the finished brief incorporated aspects of each of these approaches. At its center was the *Classic* ruling itself. Marshall's case depended on the Court's willingness to extend the *Classic* doctrines to Texas and the AWP. Without *Classic,* Marshall would be sent back to arguing the public versus private nature of the Texas Democratic Party, and the NAACP had been down that road before and lost. Marshall's primary contention therefore was that "the Constitution and laws of the United States as construed in *United States v. Classic* prohibit[ed] interference by [either the state or Texas Democrats] with [Smith's] right to vote in Texas Democratic Primaries." As the brief went on to explain, when the matter was properly viewed, there was essentially "no . . . difference between primary elections in Louisiana and in Texas." Both states made "primary elections 'an integral part of the procedure of choice.'" Each had laws mandating that parties choose their candidates by means of a primary election. And, in different ways, each state paid all or part of the costs of running primary elections. More to the point, in both states "the Democratic primary in fact 'effectively control[led] the choice' of Senators and Representatives." Combined with the former similarities — and drawing on the Court's ruling in *Classic* — the brief declared that the obvious "legal consequence" was that "the right to vote in Texas primary elections [was] secured by the Constitution."

Of course, this conclusion still left the large negative shadow cast over Smith's case by *Grovey v. Townsend*. In his district court ruling, Judge Kennerly had conceded that "the right to vote in a primary election which is 'by law made an integral party of the election machinery'" was a right "protected by the Federal Constitution." He just disagreed with Marshall that such were the facts in Texas — hence, he applied *Grovey* to deny Smith's petition. Marshall needed to attack the logic behind *Grovey* lest the justices agree with Kennerly and reject Smith's case, even in the face of *Classic*.

Marshall's second argument therefore directly challenged *Grovey*. The brief asserted that "new matter disclosed in the present record, destroy the factual basis for the decision in *Grovey v. Townsend*." The problem, the brief explained, was that, in *Grovey*, the Court had not "adequately described" the "nature, organization and functioning of the Democratic Party" of Texas. Instead, the justices had relied on "a general conclusion of the Supreme Court of Texas in *Bell v. Hill*" defining the Texas Democratic Party as "a voluntary association for political purposes" with the privilege of controlling its membership and, hence, who can vote in its primary elections. This was a mistake. "This Court was not bound to accept the conclusion of the Supreme Court of Texas as to the legal character of the primary election and the Democratic Party in Texas," Marshall explained, "for it is well settled that where the claim of a constitutional right is involved, this Court will review the record and find the facts independently of the state court." Instead, "this Court should have reserved to itself the right to pass upon the mixed question of law and fact involved in the decision whether the conduct of primary election officials in Texas constituted state action."

Were the current Court to review the full set of facts available in the *Smith* record but not before the *Grovey* Court, Marshall was confident that the justices would conclude that the Democratic primary was *not* "an election at which the members of an organized voluntary political association [chose] their candidates for public office."

For one thing, "any *white* elector, whether he considers himself Democrat, Republican, Communist . . . or non-partisan, may vote in the 'Democratic' primary." For another, the Texas Democrats had "no identified membership," nor did they have any "structure which would make [the party's] membership determinable." Third, and most important, the Democrats were "not organized," lacking all necessary rules, bylaws, and even elected officers by which to claim the status of private organization. In fact, "the only rules and regulations governing the Democratic Party and the Democratic primary elections [were] the election laws of the State of Texas." And "in such circumstances the legal character of the primary elections, and the status of those who conduct them, can be derived only from the one organized agency, which creates, requires, regulates and controls these elections, namely, the State of Texas." Combined with the new dictates of *Classic*, these facts demanded that *Grovey v. Townsend* be "overruled" and the Texas AWP declared an unconstitutional "disenfranchisement of 540,565 adult Negro citizens."

Underlying Marshall's argument was an unspoken, yet powerful, imperative for Supreme Court action: the Second World War. Situated against the backdrop of a war against totalitarianism, the NAACP's fight to gain the vote for Southern blacks drew enormous importance, and even legitimacy, from the inconsistency of fighting to defeat the Nazis abroad while at the same time denying African American citizens the rights of freedom at home. An internal memorandum prepared by the LDF in March 1944 expresses this reality clearly:

> This case is an effort to have the principles of the "Four Freedoms" made applicable at home. The right of a democracy to draft men is based upon the theory that they are liable to military service because they are citizens of a democracy. A man without the right to vote can not consider himself a full citizen, yet every day Negroes are being drafted into the armed forces. The hundreds of thousands of Negro members of the armed forces certainly have a right to be permitted to vote when they return and, in the meantime, to have members of their families permitted to exercise the fundamental right of citizens to vote.

And, while none of this context changed either the controlling precedents in Smith's case or the legal issues in dispute, the framing context of the war as an influence on the justices' willingness to act was key to Marshall's case.

Arrayed against Smith were the State of Texas and the Texas Democratic Party's Executive Committee. Neither named defendant filed a brief or sent legal representation to the Court. In fact, when the Court met on November 12, 1943, to hear oral arguments in the case, the only attorneys to show up were Marshall and his fellow lawyers. As a result, the justices, who were sitting "on the edge of their seats," according to the *Houston Informer*, heard only one side of the case — presented without interruption by a single question, an uncommon occurrence when arguing before the Court. Even Justice Roberts sat quietly (although with his lips closed tightly together) as William Hastie attacked his opinion for the Court in *Grovey*. At the last minute, however, the Texas attorney general, Gerald C. Mann, and the members of the Democratic Executive Committee requested permission to join the case as amici curiae. The Court granted their request and set the case for reargument on January 12, 1944.

Mann's position — outlined in his brief and his oral arguments and largely seconded by the Democratic Executive Committee's lawyer, Wright Morrow — was similar to that taken by the defendants in the lower court proceedings. As Mann saw it, the case raised two fundamental questions. First, "Is an election judge who conducts or holds a primary election for a political party in Texas a State officer"? Second, "Have the white Democrats in Texas . . . the right to determine who, or what class of people or voters shall constitute the party they desire to organize"?

As to the first question, Mann's answer was a resounding no. "While it is true that the Legislature in Texas has attempted to throw every safeguard around the primary elections held by any and all political parties who seek to nominate candidates for office, in order to preserve the purity of the ballot," Mann admitted, he insisted that this was not the same as taking control of the primary process. It was the parties that paid for the primary elections in Texas, not the state. In fact, Mann noted, "our courts held under our Constitution the Legislature could not do so." So long as this state of affairs remained unchanged, the primary would continue to be private in nature.

As to the supposed public nature of local election officials: "The highest courts in Texas have definitely held that the Chairman of the County Democratic Executive Committee is not an officer within the terms and definitions of the Constitution and laws of the State of Texas." What could be more definitive than this — the opinion of a state court of last resort on a matter of state law? The Supreme Court's application in *Grovey* of *Bell v. Hill* was, thus, both appropriate and correct.

Answering the second question, Mann argued that Smith's "contention that a political party in Texas cannot determine who shall be a member thereof" was "not tenable": "To say that any group of citizens cannot lawfully assemble and organize a political party for the purpose of nominating candidates for office would be to deprive them of the inalienable right given under the First Amendment to the Federal Constitution." If black or Mexican Texans wanted to start a party of their own, they could do so. Why should white Texans have any less right? For the courts to say otherwise, Mann concluded, was "to deny them the inalienable rights for which our forefathers fought and the principles upon which this Government [was] founded." Such had been the decision of the Supreme Court in *Grovey*, and such should be the decision here.

Before concluding, Mann raised the matter of *Classic*. Although he argued that it was not necessary "to attempt to reconcile the opinions of this court in the case of *Grovey v. Townsend* and *United States v. Classic*," Mann did so anyway, noting that "the facts in the two cases [were] so different that the opinion in one [did] not necessarily control the opinion in the other case." *Grovey* dealt with a party's power to determine its own membership. *Classic* had to do with issues of fraud in a state-run primary. As noted, in Texas the primary was neither run nor paid for by the state. So long as the purity of the ballot was maintained, the state was uninterested in a primary election's outcome. How could the facts of *Classic* be applied in this context? Clearly, Mann concluded, they could not. To do so would call into question the rights of " 'qualified electors' holding certain political beliefs in common the right to organize and select candidates to advocate those beliefs." And this, Mann noted, was nothing less than the death knell of political parties. "To give the Constitution the construction contended for by petitioners is to declare that the people intended to prohibit the organization of political parties, by the adoption of that instrument."

Given that this was clearly not the founders' intent, the Court's only proper response was to leave *Classic* where it was and to apply the appropriate precedent drawn from *Grovey.*

With the argument phase completed, the justices adjourned to decide the case — meeting in conference on January 15, 1944. This was actually the second time that the justices met to discuss the *Smith* case. In November, following the initial oral arguments, the justices had met to decide whether to grant Texas's motion to join the case as amicus. At that meeting, Chief Justice Stone, commenting on the case in general, had noted the essentially public nature of the primary process in Texas. In Texas, he observed, primary elections were administered by state officials; it was they who "registered voters" and, more important, "rejected black voters." True, they did so in direct response to the Democratic Party's rule banning black membership. However, Stone asked, "can we say that since state officials followed the Democratic party's proposal that only those who the party wants will vote, they ceased to act as state officials?" His own answer was no. Texas ran the primary "which resulted in control of an election . . . [in which] the colored man [was] denied a vote." As such, it was in violation of the Constitution. And, given the Court's ruling in *Classic*, the chief justice concluded, *Grovey v. Townsend* should be overturned. Justices Black, Douglas, and Murphy, in turn, had expressed general agreement with the chief justice's conclusions (although, later, Justice Black would toy with the idea of upholding the Texas AWP). Meanwhile, Justice Robert Jackson feared that overturning *Grovey* would open the door to many other lawsuits and counseled caution. Justice Roberts — as the author of the *Grovey* decision — unsurprisingly argued in favor of upholding it. "[The AWP] is not a state matter at all," he noted.

The justices now revisited their views in ruling on the merits of Smith's case. Working their way down the conference table, they soon realized that most of them opposed the AWP. Except for Justice Roberts, who refused to view the issue in racial terms, each viewed political restrictions on racial minorities as distasteful — if not necessarily unconstitutional. Influenced by the politics of the times, they found the traditional rationalizations for black voter exclusion increasingly unpersuasive. What was less clear, however, was which legal rationales justified *ending* such odious practices. Whereas some justices saw in *Classic* a mandate for overturning *Grovey*, others were not so sure.

Chief Justice Stone, for example, saw little reason to change his earlier views opposing Texas's white-only primary. As far as he was concerned, the second round of argument had done nothing to change his mind. "Texas['s argument] was interesting," he noted, "but places nothing new [on the table]. I still can't reconcile [the AWP] with the *Classic* case." As he had noted in the earlier conference, in California the state worked through private agents in enforcing its oil production rules, yet this arrangement did not make such actions private. Why should Texas's similar actions be private in this instance? "[The Texas primary] does not cease to be state action because of the Democratic party and so forth," the chief justice contended. "The colored man is denied a vote. It is an exclusion from the election. It violates the Constitution of the United States. We have reached the conclusion that the primary is an election, this being state action. I cannot reconcile this case with the *Classic* case." With "more facts" before them than had been available when the Court ruled in *Grovey*, the Chief Justice therefore called for a complete reversal of *Grovey* declaring the AWP unconstitutional.

Joining Stone was Justice Stanley Reed, who contended that black voting rights "were abridged in the majority as well as the minority party" by the Texas rules. "We must overrule [*Grovey v. Townsend*]; *Classic* did it [implicitly], now we should do it clearly." Justice Wiley Rutledge also agreed, noting that the primary in Texas "was an election" and, as such, was subject to the limits imposed by *Classic*. Justice Felix Frankfurter, on the other hand, was not fully convinced that *Classic* mandated such action — at least at first. "Like the Ku Klux Klan," he noted, "the primary system" in Texas was undoubtedly a means of "bypassing political will." Yet did that fact make "these institutions . . . unconstitutional"? His answer was a reluctant no. True, he noted, they were "Un-American," but this did not necessarily make them unconstitutional. Frankfurter therefore initially counseled caution in overturning the *Grovey* precedent. As the discussion continued, however, his views radically changed. By the end of the conference, Frankfurter had cast off his doubts and came to argue strongly in favor of declaring the Texas AWP unconstitutional. He did so on policy rather than constitutional grounds. Texas's "primary system," he contended, was a system for "bypassing [the] political will" of the people, and the Court should, therefore, construct a strongly worded opinion — one "without any pussyfooting" — overturning *Grovey* and making clear that "the Court had changed its views not on any new facts or any new factors but solely on different notions of policy from those which determined the *Grovey v. Townsend* decision."

Also concerned with the constitutional and practical implications of overturning the AWP was Justice Jackson. Constitutionally, Jackson was "not sure that this primary [was] an election." If it *was* an election, then the Court could act. If it was *not* an election, "then you can't have control over it." People had a full right to "form groups" of their choice, he argued. Only the necessity of a fair election could trump this right. But which was the case here? On a more practical level, Jackson was also troubled by the possibility that the federal courts might be permanently taking on the task of supervising state elections. In the end, however, Jackson allowed the other justices to convince him to act. In particular, Stone changed Jackson's mind when he countered: "I am not talking about all primaries, but their [Texas's] primary." It was at this point, in fact, that Justice Rutledge had joined in with his views that "*this* primary was an election" (emphasis added). On the basis that the decision would be limited to just the Texas context, and convinced by his fellow justices' views as to the public nature of the Texas primary, Jackson voted in favor of ending the Texas AWP.

Opposing the majority was Justice Roberts. As the author of *Grovey*, Roberts argued to affirm the lower court's acceptance of the AWP. In fact, clearly irritated by the challenge to his *Grovey* opinion, he did so with a blunt "I affirm," refusing even to argue the matter. Roberts was joined in this position, at least initially, by Justices Black and, as noted, Jackson. In the end, however, both Black and Jackson voted to overturn *Grovey* and declare the Texas AWP unconstitutional, leaving Roberts in lonely dissent.

With a clear majority in place, Chief Justice Stone faced the task of assigning the job of writing an opinion for the Court to one of the eight justices in the majority. His initial choice was Justice Frankfurter, who was due the assignment of writing an opinion "according to the usual procedures." Within a day, however, Stone was convinced to change his mind and transfer the assignment to Justice Reed, a Kentucky Democrat. The impetus for this change lay with Justice Jackson. Jackson was worried that an opinion written by Frankfurter would cause problems in the South. Meeting with Frankfurter in chambers, Jackson — who was personally friendly with Frankfurter — explained his concerns. According to a memorandum later written by Justice Frankfurter, among those concerns was

> that it was a very great mistake to have me [Frankfurter] write the *Allwright* opinion. For a good part of the country the subject — Negro disenfranchisement—was in the domain of the irrational and we have to take account of such facts. At best it will be very unpalatable to the South and should not be exacerbated by having the opinion written by a member of the Court who has, from the point of view of Southern prejudice, three disqualifications: "You are a New Englander, you are a Jew and you are not a Democrat — at least not recognized as such."

It would be better for either the chief justice himself or one of the Court's Southern members to write the opinion, Jackson concluded.

Justice Reed, therefore, took on the difficult task of explaining why the Court was overturning a precedent just nine years old as it decided *Smith v. Allwright* in Smith's favor. He began by noting: "Texas is free to conduct her elections and limit her electorate as she may deem wise, save only as her action may be affected by the prohibitions of the United States Constitution or in conflict with powers delegated to and exercised by the National Government." The question before the Court, therefore, was whether the Texas primary fell under the scope of federal law. In particular, did the exclusion of blacks from the Democratic primaries meet the state-action requirements imposed by the Fourteenth and Fifteenth Amendments, or was it, as the state argued, merely the private action of a private association beyond the purview of federal law?

Reed accepted that, "when *Grovey v. Townsend* was written, the Court looked upon the denial of a vote in a primary as a mere refusal by a party of party membership" and, hence, beyond the reach of federal law. Yet he doubted that this was still the case. Since *Grovey* had been decided, other cases relating to these questions had come before the Court. Among these cases was *United States v. Classic*, in which the justices held: "§ 4 of Article I of the Constitution authorized Congress to regulate primary as well as general elections, 'where the primary is by law made an integral part of the election machinery.'" And, Reed continued, *Classic* changed everything.

"The fusing by the *Classic* case of the primary and general elections into a single instrumentality for choice of officers," Reed wrote for the Court, had "a definite bearing on the permissibility under the Constitution of excluding Negroes from primaries." He continued in uncompromising terms: "The *Classic* case cuts directly into the rationale of *Grovey v. Townsend* . . . not because exclusion of Negroes from primaries is any more or less state action by reason of the unitary character of the electoral process but because the recognition of the place of the primary in the electoral scheme makes clear that state delegation to a party of the power to fix the qualifications of primary elections is delegation of a state function that may make the party's action the action of the State." Given that the "Louisiana statutes for holding primaries are similar to those of Texas," Reed explained, "our ruling in *Classic* as to the unitary character of the electoral process calls for a reexamination as to whether or not the exclusion of Negroes from a Texas party primary was state action."

Pointing to *Bell v. Hill* and *Grovey*, Texas had argued that the answer to this question was already settled in the negative and need not be reopened. Reed disagreed: "Despite Texas' decision that the exclusion is produced by private or party action, . . . federal courts must for themselves appraise the facts leading to that conclusion. It is only by the performance of this obligation that a final and uniform interpretation can be given to the Constitution, the 'supreme Law of the Land.'" And, once the question was reexamined, Reed contended, the conclusion that the Texas primary violated the Constitution was unavoidable.

As Reed saw it, where a "statutory system for the selection of party nominees for inclusion on the general election ballot" was imposed on the parties, as was the case in Texas, this made the party into an agency of the state — at least insofar as it came to running the primaries. "The party takes its character as a state agency from the duties imposed upon it by state statutes," Justice Reed wrote. Consequently, "the duties do not become matters of private law because they are performed by a political party." Despite some superficial differences, the Texas primaries mirrored those of Louisiana. True, in Louisiana, the state paid the cost of running the primaries, while, in Texas, they did not. Yet Texas statutes fixed the fees charged to run the election. The result was the same. "Whether paid directly by the State or through state requirements," Justice Reed noted, "it is state action which compels." This was the determining factor. For, "when primaries become a part of the machinery for choosing officials, state and national, . . . the same tests to determine the character of discrimination or abridgement should be applied to the primary as are applied to the general election": "If the State requires a certain electoral procedure, prescribes a general election ballot made up of party nominees so chosen and limits the choice of the electorate in general elections for state offices, practically speaking, to those whose names appear on such a ballot, it endorses, adopts and enforces the discrimination against Negroes, practiced by a party entrusted by Texas law with the determination of the qualifications of participants in the primary. This is state action within the meaning of the Fifteenth Amendment." "The United States is a constitutional democracy," Reed stressed. "Its organic law grants to all citizens a right to participate in the choice of elected officials without restriction by any State because of race." Reed insisted that the Constitution's guaranteeing the people "the opportunity for choice" could not be "nullified by a State through casting its electoral process in a form which permits a private organization to practice racial discrimination in the election." "Constitutional rights," he concluded, "would be of little value if they could be thus indirectly denied."

Mindful of the dissent that Justice Roberts was sure to pen, Reed acknowledged that, ruling as it did, the Court was ignoring its own past precedents. "We are not unmindful of the desirability of continuity of decision in constitutional questions," he wrote. Doctrinal continuity, however, could not outweigh the Court's duty to apply the Constitution's provisions faithfully — even in the face of contrary precedents. "When convinced of former error," Reed declared, "this Court has never felt constrained to follow precedent." In fact, when it came to "constitutional questions, where correction depends upon amendment and not upon legislative action this Court throughout its history has freely exercised its power to reexamine the basis of its constitutional decisions. This has long been accepted practice, and this practice has continued to this day. This is particularly true when the decision believed erroneous is the application of a constitutional principle rather than an interpretation of the Constitution to extract the principle itself."

At root, therefore, Reed was arguing that all the justices were doing was reexamining the facts of the Texas primary in the light of the

Court's deeper understanding of the Constitution's provisions as shaped by *Classic*. *Classic*, in turn, had set out two tests to determine whether a primary was, in fact, a part of the electoral process and, thus, protected by the Fourteenth and Fifteenth Amendments: first, was the primary "an integral part of the election machinery"; second, did its outcome significantly affect who was elected. In both cases, Reed explained, the Texas primaries met these burdens. Once this fact was established, the right of a private organization to determine its membership as it saw fit, held in *Grovey* to be pertinent, was no longer of practical relevance. By integrating the Democratic Party into its electoral process, Texas had made this party into a quasi-public agency subject to federal regulations, and federal law prohibited the exclusion of voters on account of race or color. As Justice Reed concluded: "Here we are applying, contrary to the recent decision in *Grovey v. Townsend*, the well-established principle of the Fifteenth Amendment, forbidding the abridgement by a State of a citizen's right to vote. *Grovey v. Townsend* is overruled."

Not all the justices were happy with Reed's handling of *Smith v. Allwright*. Justice Frankfurter, who approved of the case's outcome, felt that Reed had not been candid enough in explaining the reasons for overturning *Grovey*. Reed implied that the Court was overturning *Grovey*, not because the justices necessarily disagreed with the logic of that decision, but because their deeper understandings of the Constitution produced by their decision in *Classic* made *Grovey* largely irrelevant. Frankfurter felt that such "legal pussy-footing and petty-fogging" was a mistake. *Grovey* was overturned because the justices felt that it was wrong. As Frankfurter had noted in conference, he felt that "the Court had changed its views not on any new facts or any new factors but solely on different notions of policy from those which determined the *Grovey v. Townsend* decision." Frustrated, Frankfurter penned a concurring opinion strongly stating his views that "no mere individual preference but only a compelling regard for the Constitution as a dynamic scheme of government for a democratic society can justify a different conclusion from that reached in *Grovey v. Townsend*." In the end, however, Frankfurter decided not to publish this draft concurrence. Concerned that any hint of disagreement on the part of those justices backing the *Smith* ruling might undermine its effectiveness, Frankfurter merely concurred with Justice Reed's opinion but did not explain why or how his views differed from those of the majority.

More serious was the anger of Justice Roberts. As the author of the opinion for the Court in *Grovey*, Roberts saw Reed's opinion as a direct and personal attack on himself and his constitutional judgment. "I have expressed my views [elsewhere] with respect to the present policy of the court freely to disregard and to overrule considered decisions and the rules of law announced in them," Roberts wrote. "This tendency, it seems to me, indicates an intolerance for what those who have composed this court in the past have conscientiously and deliberately concluded, and involves an assumption that knowledge and wisdom reside in us which was denied to our predecessors."

*Grovey*, Roberts declared, "received the attention and consideration which the questions involved demanded and the opinion represented the views of all the justices." Yet, sadly, "it appears that those views do not now commend themselves to the court." So be it. If the majority wanted to argue that *Classic* had overturned *Grovey* "sub silentio" without ever having mentioned *Grovey* once, then there was little that Roberts could do about it. He wished only that, "if this court's opinion in the *Classic* case" disclosed a new "method of overruling earlier decisions," the Court "in fairness . . . should . . . have adopted" this method in an "open and frank way of saying what it was doing," rather than, after the event, "characteriz[ing] its past action as overruling *Grovey v. Townsend* though those less sapient never realized the fact."

The soundness of *Grovey* or *Classic*, however, was "not a matter which presently concerns me," Roberts explained. Rather, "my concern is that the instant decision, overruling that announced about nine years ago, tends to bring adjudications of this tribunal into the same class as a restricted railroad ticket, good for this day and train only. I have no assurance, in view of current decisions, that the opinion announced today may not shortly be repudiated and overruled by justices who deem they have new light on the subject." Such transience was wrong. It undermined the very foundations of the law. It was also bad for the nation: "It is regrettable that in an era marked by doubt and confusion, an era whose greatest need is steadfastness of thought and purpose, this court, which has been looked to as exhibiting consistency in adjudication, and a steadiness which would hold the balance even in the face of temporary ebbs and flows of opinion, should now itself become the breeder of fresh doubt and confusion in the public mind as to the stability of our institutions."

Roberts's heated and angry dissent generated ill will on the part of some of the other justices. Justice Rutledge, in particular, drafted a concurrence that he never circulated expressing his frustration with opinions that "cast aspersions on the integrity of those who 'depart[ed] from accepted bases of judicial action.'" On the whole, however, the justices kept their disagreements private. Disagreements about constitutional justifications were generally overshadowed by the majority's consensus that the Texas AWP had to go. It was with an almost unanimous face, therefore, that the Court faced the world when it announced its *Smith* ruling on April 3, 1944. The Texas AWP was declared judicially dead by the highest court in the United States. The only question was whether this declaration would have any more lasting impact than the Court's earlier efforts to dismantle the AWP.

CHAPTER 6

---

# Death Knell

## The All-White Primary after *Smith*

July 28, 1944. Accompanied by friends and reporters, Dr. Lonnie Smith arrived early at the Eighty-fourth Precinct, near his home in northeast Houston, and cast his ballot in the Democratic Party's primary election. Citywide, 2,618 Houston blacks joined Smith in exercising their franchise. Statewide, the number of African American voters who took part in the primary stood in the low tens of thousands. (As the deadline for the payment of poll taxes had already passed by the time the Supreme Court's ruling was announced in April, only those blacks who had already paid could vote in this election, which limited the number of potential black voters.) Despite fears that the Democrats would find a way — once again — to resurrect the all-white primary (AWP), the 1944 primary election went off without a major hitch. In Houston, only one precinct judge threatened to continue the ban on black voting — and even he relented on election day. Almost twenty years to the day since Dr. Lawrence A. Nixon had sought to vote in the El Paso Democratic primary, the Texas AWP seemed to be, not only merely dead, but really most sincerely dead.

Across the nation, the black press trumpeted the AWP's demise loudly. The *Chicago Defender* on April 15 described the victory as a "milestone in the battle to fully integrate Negroes into the mainstream of American life" (although the paper did warn: "We cannot expect its full effect to be immediately felt"). The *Houston Informer* agreed, noting that the justices' decision vindicated twenty years of argument and struggle by Texas blacks. Thurgood Marshall also declared in correspondence and public speeches that the ruling was "so clear and free of ambiguity" that it settled "once and for all the question of the right of Negroes to participate in primary elections similar to those in Texas." In an April 18 interview with the *Informer,* Lonnie

Smith himself noted that he felt "about like all other Negroes in Texas and the South, . . . happy to be able to vote and see Negroes free in the real sense of the word."

Yet how dead was the AWP? Although some Southern whites were willing to end the fight and accept black voting in the primaries, others were adamant that the ban be continued or reestablished. In Texas, for instance, the *Dallas Times Herald* provisionally — if unhappily — accepted the Supreme Court's *Smith* ruling, calling on white Texans to do nothing "that might be construed as contempt of that august body," but the neighboring *Fort Worth Star-Telegram* attacked the decision, arguing: "It was safe to assume that the Democratic party in the South will remain a 'white man's' party and that Texas, against which the newest and most formidable challenge is directed, will devise the pattern by which this status will be retained." The Texas State Bar Association adopted a resolution attacking the Court's decision in *Smith* and arguing: "The Supreme Court of the United States is losing, if it has not already lost, the high esteem in which it has been held by the people." Weaver Moore, a state senator from Houston, even introduced a bill designed to sever all state ties to the Democratic primary and, thus, to allow the Democrats to continue privately as a whites-only party. (Governor Coke Stevenson refused to call a special legislative session, however, and the bill never came to a vote.)

Similar patterns of action and reaction reverberated throughout the South. Mississippi Democratic Executive Committee Chairman Herbert Holmes, for example, condemned the decision and asserted: "We still have a few State's rights left, and one of our rights is to have Democratic primaries and say who shall vote in them." Neither the "Supreme Court" nor anyone else, he declared, "can control a Democratic primary in Mississippi." In Congress, Senator Bernet Maybank of South Carolina warned: "The white people of the South will not accept these interferences. We are proud of our section. We know what is best for the white people and the colored people. We are going to treat the Negro fairly, but in so doing we do not intend for him to take over our election system or attend our white schools. Regardless of any Supreme Court decision or any laws that may be passed by Congress, we of the South will maintain our political and social institutions as we believe to be in the best interests of our people." Mississippi Senator James O. Eastland agreed, complaining that the ruling showed "an alarming tendency to destroy State sovereignty." Meanwhile, John H. Overton, a senator from Louisiana, cautioned (in words that hinted of events to come): "We're not going to submit to Negro voting in our elections. . . . We don't need white primaries, or poll taxes. We can keep them out on educational qualifications."

In fact, whereas white response in the outer tier of Southern states was generally—if grudgingly—accepting, in the Deep South, where most blacks lived, opposition to *Smith* was widespread and intense. Deeply concerned over the perilous implications for Jim Crow segregation of allowing blacks to vote, white Southerners in the Deep South refused to accept the inevitability of the AWP's demise. It had been resurrected before in the face of Supreme Court interference; it could be resurrected again. The result was a varied and often potent effort to retain the essence of the AWP in states across the South. The nature of these efforts varied from state to state. In some states, formal legislative action sought to retain as much of the AWP as possible. In others, informal action by Democrats challenged *Smith*'s effectiveness. In the end, none of these efforts to retain the AWP succeeded. However, in the process of implementing this effort, Southerners adopted and expanded other more extreme efforts at vote denial. The result, as we shall see, gave the AWP's defeat an ambiguous quality.

The campaign to undermine *Smith* started within hours of the announcement of the High Court's ruling in *Smith v. Allwright.* Although Justice Reed's opinion for the Court was the justices' strongest statement in favor of black voting to date, it still left important questions unresolved. The foremost of these was whether state action was *required* for federal jurisdiction, and, hence, protection, to arise. One National Association for the Advancement of Colored People (NAACP) attorney prepared a staff memorandum on April 5, 1944, analyzing Reed's opinion. On the one hand, the memorandum pointed out, the opinion held "that barring a person from a primary election on account of color or race [was] a depravation of a constitutional right regardless of how that result [was] achieved." On the other hand, Reed seemed to be basing much of his judgment on the *link* between state law and party action. As the NAACP memorandum rephrased Reed's words, "the party takes its character as a state agency from the duties imposed upon it by state statutes," and, given that Texas "made the privilege of membership in a party the essential qualification for voting in the primary," it was this mandate that "constituted state action." Yet what if the link between state law and party action were severed? Would *Smith* apply if a primary were truly private in nature? As the memorandum warned: "This language concerning the statutory scheme in Texas and what is and is not state action may open the door for the invention of new contrivances to bar Negroes from voting in primary elections."

The NAACP staff attorney who wrote this memorandum was not the only one to see this potential hidden within the *Smith* ruling. In a speech given the same day that the NAACP memorandum was written, Florida Senator Claude Pepper argued that "in Florida not the State but the Democratic party determines the qualifications of members of the party" and that, if, per chance, "there is any question about . . . our statute," "it can be altered and the matter left exclusively in the hands of the party of determining who may vote in the Democratic primary. This can be done and the Democratic primaries kept white under the decision of the Supreme Court." Privatization, then, was *Smith*'s Achilles heel — or so Southern whites hoped.

The first effort to test the exclusionary potential of privatization arose in South Carolina. Less than two weeks after the Supreme Court announced its *Smith* ruling, Governor Olin D. Johnston called for a special session of the South Carolina General Assembly to respond to *Smith*. Johnston himself vehemently objected to the Court's undermining of the AWP. Speaking soon after the justices handed down their decision, Johnston declared: "History has taught us that we must keep our white primaries pure and unadulterated so that we might protect the welfare of all people in our state." Outside interference would not change this fundamental fact. "White Supremacy," he proclaimed, "will be maintained in our primaries. Let the chips fall where they may!" It was up to the legislature to make this boast a reality.

Johnston's proposal to the legislature built on the assumption that *Smith* depended for its constitutional authority on the state's control of the primary process. Separate the state from the primary process, Johnston reasoned, and *Smith* no longer applied. Agreeing with this logic, the legislature repealed all its primary-election laws and amendments. Working with extreme care, and fearful that even a single primary-election law on the books would be enough for the courts to apply

*Smith* to South Carolina, the legislators did not even trust the statute book's index. Instead, they "turned the statute books page by page . . . to find out if anything was there that wasn't properly indexed." By the time they finished, the assembly had repealed approximately 150 separate laws and regulations. Five months later, the people of South Carolina approved an amendment removing all mention of primary elections from the state constitution.

Georgia Democrats' first reaction to *Smith* was to declare that the Texas primary case did not apply to them. Consequently, in July 1944, the state Democratic Executive Committee ordered county election judges to continue to bar blacks from the polls. Challenged by local blacks in the federal courts, this campaign of defiance fell in October 1945 to a ruling by U.S. District Judge T. Hoyt Davis in *King v. Chapman*. As the Fifth Circuit later affirmed, although the state did not organize or regulate the primaries, it still "collaborate[d] in the conduct of the primary, and put its power behind the rules of the party," all of which made "the primary . . . a part of the public election machinery." Georgia's response to this ruling was to follow South Carolina's lead and repeal all its primary-election laws in an effort to cut off all public aspects of the primary process.

In Florida, State Senators John E. Mathews and G. Warren Sanchez proposed a "private" primary bill to the legislature in 1945. Never voted out of committee, the bill sat in limbo as the Democratic state committee rescinded its white-primary rules — except that, in June 1946, the committee reversed course and unanimously requested the state legislature to repeal all election laws "which prevent the Democratic Party from remaining an exclusively white party." Encouraged by this and similar calls in defense of the AWP, the senators resubmitted the bill in March 1947, and it came up for a floor vote in May. Yet the highly controversial bill ultimately went down to defeat. Although many legislators were concerned with the costs of allowing blacks to vote, they were equally worried over the potential for a private primary system to lead to fraud (if the Matthews law went into effect, election fraud would not be illegal) and for the dominance of political cliques and factions. The bill's failure did Florida blacks little good, however, as informal intimidation in rural areas of the state limited the total numbers of blacks able to vote. (In one section of

Florida, blacks seeking to register to vote as Democrats received letters warning that they would "be floating up and down the river," while others had shots fired into their homes.)

Arkansas Democrats took a unique approach to keeping blacks from the primaries. Rather than privatize the primary system entirely, Arkansas party officials separated party membership from the right to vote in a primary — and then proceeded to exclude blacks from party membership. Since it was the party that nominated the candidates for the primary ballot, this meant that Arkansas blacks could vote, but only for those candidates whom the white community had already chosen. This dichotomy was made official one year later when the Arkansas legislature adopted new rules regulating primary elections. In particular, the new laws created a double-tiered primary system in which nominations for office were decided in a "preference" primary (open to whites only) and the actual candidates for office selected in a "runoff" primary open to party members *and* outsiders. Then, to add to the complexity, the new rules required separate primary elections (of both types) for state and federal office. Combined with challenges against black voters as supporters of the Republican Party (in past elections, blacks had voted Republican as their only choice and, hence, were not permitted to vote as Democrats), the result of the new system was the effective continuation of the AWP's effects without (or so the lawmakers hoped) violating the letter of the Supreme Court's ruling in *Smith*.

Interestingly, Texas, which had been at the forefront of the AWP debate for so many years, chose not to respond formally to *Smith*. Although State Senator Weaver Moore did submit a privatization bill to the Texas legislature, the lawmakers never voted on it. Perhaps, tired of the endless fighting, the formal organs of Texas government and politics gave up the struggle and passed up any chance to challenge the Court's ruling. At the local level, however, things were slightly different. In Marshall, Texas National Guardsmen were stationed at the polls to intimidate black voters during the 1946 primaries. Although they were withdrawn after black leaders asked each guardsman to sign affidavits attesting that he was stationed specifically to exclude black voters, the use of intimidation was real. In Colorado County, election officials separated the ballots for state and local office and then gave both ballots to white voters but only the state ballot to blacks. Waxahachie officials excluded black voters from the polls when it became apparent that more blacks than whites had paid their poll taxes.

The strongest efforts to retain the essence of the AWP in Texas arose in Fort Bend County, however. During the conflicts of the late nineteenth century, Fort Bend County whites had organized themselves politically under the banner of the all-white Jaybird Democratic Association. One of many white men's unions to form in East Texas, the Jaybirds held unofficial "preprimaries" as a means to undermine black voting. Whereas most of these white men's unions died out by the early twentieth century, the Jaybird primary survived. By 1950, when black residents of Fort Bend County challenged the Jaybird primary, membership in the association was automatically open to all whites registered to vote in Fort Bend County. Usually, the Jaybirds would hold their preprimary a few weeks before the official Democratic primary; those seeking county office would make their case to the white community. The winners of this "informal" polling would, in turn, seek a place on the ballot in Democratic primaries. Although no pledge of support followed from a victory in the Jaybird primary, the persons endorsed in the Jaybird primary normally were the only persons whose names would appear on the official primary ballot. As such, these nominees were almost always elected or nominated in the official Democratic primary. Given that the Democratic nominees were almost always victorious in the general election, an endorsement in the Jaybird primary essentially guaranteed success in the general election in November. Following *Smith*, the Jaybird primary took on added significance as Fort Bend County whites searched for a way to prevent blacks from participating in the political process.

Efforts such as these posed serious challenges to *Smith*'s effectiveness. If merely making the primary private was enough to preclude federal enforcement, then *Smith* was useless. African Americans had been down that road before. Still, encouraged by the victory in *Smith*, the NAACP — now with the help of the federal government — moved against these renewed exclusionary voting practices both politically and legally in the federal courts.

The first target was Georgia's attempt to ignore *Smith* by simply claiming that, as Georgia and Texas primary-election laws were different, *Smith* did not reach Georgia's Democratic primaries. *King v. Chapman* came before U.S. District Judge T. Hoyt Davis in October

1945. At issue was *Smith*'s reach beyond the Texas context. The plaintiffs argued that the *Smith* ruling should be applied widely across the South; the defendants maintained the alternative. Ruling on October 12, Judge Davis sided with the plaintiffs; he ruled that Georgia's primary elections were "by law an integral part of the electoral process of the State of Georgia," which made the "holding of said primary [an] action by the State of Georgia, acting through the Democratic Party as its instrumentality." Given that the plaintiffs' right to vote in a primary election was a "right secured to [them] by the Constitution and laws of the United States," the judge explained, the Democratic Party's refusal "to permit plaintiff to vote in said primary election solely on account of his race and color" constituted a deprivation of "a right secured to [plaintiffs] by the Constitution and laws of the United States, . . . in violation of the Fourteenth, Fifteenth and Seventeenth Amendments."

On appeal, a three-judge panel of the Fifth Circuit affirmed Judge Davis's ruling on the grounds that the state "collaborates in the conduct of the primary, . . . puts its power behind the rules of the party . . . [and, thus,] adopts the primary as a part of the public election machinery." Consequently, the panel held, any "exclusions of voters made by the party by the primary rules become" by legal definition "exclusions enforced by the State" subject to federal protections.

The next state's primary to face legal challenge after *Smith* was South Carolina's privatization effort. With the Democratic primary now privatized by legislative action, party officials were determined to exclude black voters from the 1946 primary; South Carolina blacks were equally determined not to allow this to happen. With the arrival of the August primaries, these two perspectives came into conflict. When blacks from Columbia, South Carolina, attempted to vote in Richland County's Ninth Ward precinct, they were turned away. In response, they filed a class action suit against the county Democratic committee. Thurgood Marshall and the NAACP's Legal Defense and Education Fund would have preferred to leave prosecution of such matters to the Justice Department, but, for political reasons, the federal government refused to act. Consequently, Marshall took on the case, prepared to challenge the legitimacy of South Carolina's privatization efforts.

Appearing before U.S. District Judge J. Waties Waring, Marshall drew heavily on *Classic*'s determination that primary elections were subject to constitutional protections where "state law . . . made the primary an integral part of the procedure of choice, or where in fact [it] effectively control[ed] the choice" of candidates. As Marshall saw it, these two requirements were *alternative* tests for determining whether a primary came under federal regulation. "The two tests set forth so clearly in the *Classic* case," his brief for the Court noted, "are in the *alternative*." As such, "under the *Classic* case, the plaintiff in this case is entitled to recover where either" condition was met. And, whereas the South Carolina Democratic primary no longer was regulated under state law, in a one-party state where the Democrats always won the general election, it still clearly controlled the choice of candidates.

The defendants moved to dismiss the complaint, stressing the need for a strict reading of the Supreme Court's precedents. In both *Classic* and *Smith* — in fact, in every case that deemed primaries subject to federal law — the primaries challenged were regulated by state law. "In all those cases," the defendants insisted, "the Democratic primary was by statute made an essential part of the statutory electoral process." Such was no longer the case in South Carolina. The revision of the state's election laws changed everything. The Democratic Party of South Carolina was now nothing more than a private club, similar in structure (if not size) to a sewing circle or a country club. As such, the precedents "must be held to sustain the proposition that where, as here, the primary [was] no part of the statutory process of an election . . . there [was] no Constitutional right to vote in such primary."

On July 12, 1947, Judge Waring announced his decision in *Elmore v. Rice*. A native of South Carolina with liberal leanings, Waring was deeply troubled by the implications (to say nothing of the effects) of the state's efforts to maintain the AWP. Consequently, he declared unconstitutional South Carolina's attempt to rewrite its election laws to "completely renounce control of political parties and [the] primaries held there under." Such efforts to divorce party primaries from state authority and, thus, continue the prohibition on black voting in the Democratic primary, Waring held, were inventive but not constitutionally sufficient. Despite the rule changes, "the present Democratic Party in South Carolina is acting for and on behalf of the people of South Carolina." It was not the same as a ladies' sewing circle. "Private clubs and business organizations do not vote and elect a President of the United States," he explained, or "Senators and members of the House of Representatives of our national congress." More to the point, "under the law of our land, all citizens are entitled to a voice in such selections." This simple reality was the controlling factor. "All citizens of this State and Country are entitled to cast a free and untrammeled ballot in our elections," Waring declared, "and if the only material and realistic elections are clothed with the name 'primary,' they are equally entitled to vote there." It was "time for South Carolina to rejoin the Union," he concluded, "time to fall in step with the other states and to adopt the American way of conducting elections."

When the defendants appealed Judge Waring's decision, a three-judge panel of the Fourth Circuit asked "whether, by permitting a party to take over a part of its election machinery, a state can avoid the provisions of the Constitution forbidding racial discrimination in elections and can deny to a part of the electorate, because of race and color, any effective voice in the government of the state." The judges answered no. "The fundamental error in defendant's position," Judge John J. Parker explained for the panel, "consists in the premise that a political party is a mere private aggregation of individuals, like a country club, and that the primary is a mere piece of party machinery. The party may, indeed, have been a mere private aggregation of individuals in the early days of the Republic, but with the passage of the years, political parties have become in effect state institutions, governmental agencies through which sovereign power is exercised by the people." Given that "the use of the Democratic primary in connection with the general election in South Carolina provides . . . [an] election machinery for that state" and that "the denial to the Negro of the right to participate in the primary denies him all effective voice in the government of his country," there could be "no question that such denial amounts to a denial of the constitutional rights of the Negro" subject to the protection of the courts. The panel therefore affirmed Judge Waring's ruling and its underlying reasoning.

Despite these judicial defeats, South Carolina remained committed to retaining the essence of the AWP. Following their defeat in *Elmore*, South Carolina Democrats adopted new membership rules permitting blacks to vote in the primary but excluding them from party membership. All nonmembers participating in a primary vote were, in turn, required to affirm under oath their support of states' rights and segregation and to note their opposition to federal fair employment rules before they could vote. Confident that no blacks would truthfully admit "to believ[ing] in . . . the social . . . and educational separation of races" and "in the principles of States' Rights," South Carolina Democrats anticipated that these machinations would meet the needs of Judge Waring's *Elmore* ruling while minimizing black voting.

Acting quickly, Marshall sought in July 1948 an injunction blocking all such efforts to exclude black voters. His justification was simple. Given the practical outcome of full enforcement of the new rules — the exclusion of black voters from the Democratic primary — these rules were nothing more than a deliberate attempt to subvert the spirit of the *Elmore* ruling. As such, he concluded, they were an illegal deprivation of voting rights based exclusively on race.

Argued before Judge Waring in July and November 1948, the questions before the court in *Brown v. Baskin*, as the case came to be titled, were "quite narrow," most of the issues having been settled in *Elmore*. The only issue needing determination, as Judge Waring explained, was whether "the oath which was adopted by the convention [was an] attempt to evade the American principle of allowing all persons to freely exercise the suffrage" or merely the proper exercise of the party's powers of organization over its membership and voting procedures. To the latter option, Judge Waring answered no. "The action of the Democratic State Convention in May 1948," he noted, was "in direct contradiction of all law and custom, which must or should have been well known to any students or even casual inquirers in regard to such matters." *Elmore* was conclusive, Judge Waring explained, that " 'the plaintiff and others similarly situated are entitled to be enrolled and to vote in the primaries conducted by the Democratic Party of South Carolina.' " Consequently, "such a flagrant disregard of basic rights must have sprung from either gross ignorance or a conscious determination to evade the issue and to refuse to obey the law of the land." Given the wide experience and legal knowledge of those individuals who made up the convention, the judge could conclude only "that the action of the convention was a deliberate attempt to evade the apparent consequence of the *Elmore* case," namely, "the American principle of allowing all persons to freely exercise the suffrage." Waring therefore ruled that to "require, as a prerequisite to voting, that qualified electors take an oath subscribing to the views of the State Convention and/or its Executive Committee, is a flagrant disregard of the rights of American citizens to exercise their own views and opinions in the choice of representatives in their national government" and, hence, unconstitutional.

Angered by the party's attempt to subvert his *Elmore* ruling, Judge Waring refused to let the matter end. Instead, he lectured the defendants about the error of their ways. "Neither in South Carolina nor in any other State in this union," he declared, "have American citizens as yet come to a pass where a group of party officials, in violation of basic American rights, can prescribe oaths, methods and a code of thought for voters." If one were to carry this thought pattern "to its logical conclusion," Waring complained, "it is wondered why the State Convention did not require an oath that all parties enrolling or voting should elect them in perpetuity and with satisfactory emoluments." For a political party to claim a right "not only to segregate according to race, to prescribe different methods of gaining the right to vote, to forbid participation in the organization for government of the party, but [also] to prescribe mental tests and set up a code of thought which, far from being a bill of rights, might rather he called a bill of persecutions," was wrong. It was also something that the court would not allow to continue. "It is important that once and for all, the members of this Party be made to understand — and that is the purpose of this opinion — that they will be required to obey and carry out the orders of this court, not only in the technical respects but in the true spirit and meaning of the same," Waring declared. "It is time that either the present officials of the Party, or such as may be in the future chosen, realize that the people of the United States expect them to follow the American way of elections" and that the Democratic Party primaries "be freely open to all parties entitled to enter therein under the laws and Constitution of this country and State, without discrimination of race, color or creed." Then, lest his point be missed, Waring warned that "any violation of the terms of the Order, or of the law as set forth in this opinion, . . . will be considered a contempt and will be proceeded against and punished."

On appeal to the Fourth Circuit, Judge Waring's decision was again upheld. Writing for the Court, Judge Parker noted: "By requiring of voters in the primaries an oath which would effectually exclude

Negroes, those in control of the Democratic Party [were] attempting to do by indirection that which . . . they could not do [directly]. . . . The devices adopted showed plainly the unconstitutional purpose for which they were designed; but, even if they had appeared to be innocent, they should be enjoined if their purpose or effect is to discriminate against voters on account of race." The circuit judges thus saw "no reason to modify [their] holding in *Rice v. Elmore*." In fact, "on the contrary, [they were] convinced, after further consideration, that the decision in that case was entirely correct." South Carolina's AWP was dead.

In Texas, as fate would have it, what would be the final word on the private nature of primaries and of the AWP's legitimacy arose from a challenge to the Texas Jaybirds and their attempt to hold an exclusive "informal primary" before the formal integrated one. This case ultimately came before the Supreme Court and gave that body the chance to compose a final accounting of the AWP's unconstitutionality.

Following *Smith*, the Jaybird "preprimary" provided a means by which local whites in Texas could exclude blacks from political power despite blacks' capacity to vote in the Democratic primaries. Members of the local black community who saw the Jaybird primary as the AWP by another name not only resented it but, by 1949, replaced resentment with action. Turning to a local white attorney, J. Edwin Smith, after the NAACP's local branch refused to participate in a civil suit (as Smith recalled, the NAACP feared the negative effects of losing), the black community filed suit against the Jaybirds. The lawsuit maintained that the Jaybirds were, in effect, a political party the sole purpose of which was to deny Negro voters any voice in the political process. In response, the Jaybirds portrayed themselves as merely a private association of white citizens with the sole objective of securing to the people of Fort Bend County "economic and honest county government and the election of honest and faithful county officials."

Filed with the Southern District Court of Texas in late 1949, the case of *Terry v. Adams* came to trial in March 1950. Ironically, the case came before Judge Thomas Kennerly, the same judge who a decade earlier had ruled against Dr. Smith and affirmed the Texas AWP. Despite his history of support for the AWP, Judge Kennerly now held the segregated Jaybird Democratic Association to be "a political organization or party" and noted "that its chief object had always been

to deny Negroes any voice or part in the election of county officials."
Judge Kennerly was as uncompromising in his opinion rejecting the
Jaybird primary as he had been a decade before in rejecting Dr.
Smith's original lawsuit: "I do not agree with Defendants' contention
that such Association is not a political party, nor that it is not regulated by the Laws of Texas, nor that it is not an agency of the State.
Such Association is a political party and comes clearly within the
[reach of state statute] which regulates it and makes it an agency of
the State. . . . Such Association cannot avoid the effect of [state law]
by holding its primaries on a date different from the date fixed by such
Article, nor by different methods." Judge Kennerly therefore ruled
the association's racial discriminations invalid and entered judgment
accordingly.

A three-judge panel of the Fifth Circuit Court of Appeals disagreed
with Judge Kennerly's description of the Jaybird Democratic Association as a "political party." Writing for the panel, Judge Joseph Hutcheson (who also had ruled against Dr. Smith in favor of the AWP)
argued in *Adams v. Terry* that the Jaybirds were *not* a political party.
"The Jaybird Democratic Association does not in any way or manner
operate as a part or parcel of, or in liaison with, state political or elective machinery," he insisted. "In short, it is not a part of the two step
arrangement, the Democratic primary and the general election, so as
to make its action state action." Hutcheson acknowledged that "it
[was] true that in the main . . . the endorsement of the Jaybird primary does usually mean that the winner of that endorsement will have
no opposition in the Democratic primary." Yet this did not make the
Jaybirds into a political party, nor did it make its proceedings state
action under the Fourteenth and Fifteenth Amendments. How could
a vote that had no legal or binding effect be deemed public in any way,
Hutcheson asked? The Jaybird candidates won "because, and only because, there [was] a consensus of opinion in the country that the endorsement should be regarded as decisive." Hutcheson was willing to
admit that, if "the question for our decision were whether, from the
standpoint of good neighborliness and good government in the
changed and changing climate of opinion in this state, there [was] any
point in clinging, under the greatly different conditions now prevailing, to this outworn and outmoded shadow boxing, these mock elections, we should be constrained to declare that it seems to us that the

white voters of Fort Bend County are vainly holding to the husks of a respected tradition long after the ripe grain has fallen." Such, however, was not "our question." Accordingly, the judges ruled that there was no constitutional or congressional bar to the "admitted discriminatory exclusion of Negroes" because Jaybird primaries were not to any extent "state controlled."

When the case came before the U.S. Supreme Court in 1953, the result shifted once again. Perplexed by the case's legal complexities, and troubled by the practical implications of declaring that the Jaybirds were a public party subject to all the law's requirements, the justices struggled to find a coherent theory to overturn the Jaybird election — which, admittedly, they all found offensive. In the end, creating consensus proved an impossible task. The result was that the justices handed down multiple opinions justifying and explaining the Court's actions.

Justice Hugo L. Black, writing for himself and Justices William O. Douglas and Harold H. Burton, agreed with Judge Kennerly that the Jaybird election was the "real" primary election in Fort Bend County. Black based his opinion in the context of South Carolina's failed attempt to privatize the primary system. Black found no substantive difference between what South Carolina had attempted to do and the Jaybirds' efforts. "It is significant," he noted, "that precisely the same qualifications as those prescribed by Texas entitling electors to vote at county-operated primaries are adopted as the sole qualifications entitling electors to vote at the county-wide Jaybird primaries with a single proviso — Negroes are excluded. Everyone concedes that such a proviso in the county-operated primaries would be unconstitutional. The Jaybird Party thus brings into being and holds precisely the kind of election that the Fifteenth Amendment seeks to prevent. When it produces the equivalent of the prohibited election, the damage has been done." "For a state to permit such a duplication of its election processes [was] to permit a flagrant abuse of those processes to defeat the purposes of the Fifteenth Amendment," Black concluded. "The use of the county-operated primary to ratify the result of the prohibited election merely compounds the offense." The "official" election was, thus, a sham — nothing more "than the perfunctory ratifiers of the choice that [had] been already made in Jaybird elections." What did it matter that the state did not control the Jaybird election? The

Jaybird primary was "an integral part, indeed the only effective part, of the elective process that determines who shall rule and govern in the county." The effect of the whole procedure was, in turn, to do precisely what the Fifteenth Amendment forbade — to "strip Negroes of every vestige of influence in selecting the officials who control the local county matters that intimately touch the daily lives of citizens."

Justice Tom C. Clark (joined by Chief Justice Fred Vinson and Justices Stanley Reed and Robert H. Jackson) also supported Judge Kennerly's judgment against the Jaybirds. Clark, however, based his concurring opinion more directly on the Court's *Smith* ruling. "We agree with Chief District Judge Kennerly that the Jaybird Democratic Association is a political party whose activities fall within the Fifteenth Amendment's self-executing ban," Clark wrote. And, whereas "not every private club, association or league organized to influence public candidacies or political action must conform to the Constitution's restrictions on political parties," the Jaybirds did fall under that ban. A close reading of the record showed "that the Jaybird Democratic Association operates . . . as an auxiliary of the local Democratic Party organization, selecting its nominees and using its machinery for carrying out an admitted design of destroying the weight and effect of Negro ballots in Fort Bend County." And, although "the Democratic primary and the general election are nominally open to the colored elector, . . . this [resulted in] an empty vote cast after the real decisions are made." Whether viewed "as a separate political organization or as an adjunct of the local Democratic Party, the Jaybird Democratic Association" was, thus, "the decisive power in the county's recognized electoral process." And, "when a state structures its electoral apparatus in a form which devolves upon a political organization the uncontested choice of public officials, that organization itself, in whatever disguise, takes on those attributes of government which draw the Constitution's safeguards into play."

Speaking only for himself, Justice Frankfurter also held against the Jaybirds, but his concurring opinion's reasoning differed noticeably from either of the other opinions. Like his colleagues, Frankfurter did not want to give a judicial stamp of approval to the Jaybirds' actions, which he found questionable at best. However, he worried that the Court might go too far in regulating private organizations if it declared the Jaybirds a controlling political party subject to constitutional limitations. As he explained:

> This case is for me by no means free of difficulty. Whenever the law draws a line between permissive and forbidden conduct cases are bound to arise which are not obviously on one side or the other. These dubious situations disclose the limited utility of the figure of speech, "a line," in the law. Drawing a "line" is necessarily exercising a judgment, however confined the conscientious judgment may be within the bounds of constitutional and statutory provisions, the course of decisions, and the presuppositions of the judicial process. If "line" is in the main a fruitful tool for dividing the sheep from the goats, it must not be forgotten that since the "line" is figurative the place of this or that case in relation to it cannot be ascertained externally but is a matter of the mind.

Frankfurter worried that any judicial declaration of the Jaybirds' "public" nature could undermine the existence of this line — not just for the Jaybirds, but for all private organizations concerned with political matters. Did the public nature of the Jaybirds mean that blacks could legally force it to enroll African American members? What about religious groups? Frankfurter was unsure but was concerned about the potential unintended consequences of ruling too sweepingly against the Jaybirds.

Instead of such a broad definition of *public*, Frankfurter argued that the Court should adopt a safer approach to ending the negative effects of the Jaybird elections. As he saw it, the justices could overrule the Jaybirds' actions because the state had failed in its duty to assure a fair and equitable voting process. Texas properly had rules regulating the operations of elections, Frankfurter noted, rules in which the "county election officials [were] . . . clothed with the authority of the State to secure observance of the State's interest in 'fair methods and a fair expression' of preferences in the selection of nominees." When the Jaybirds undermined the "fairness" of the electoral process and the local officials did nothing to halt this process, in fact helping it along, the state by definition failed in its duty to assure a fair and equitable voting process. "This is not a case of occasional efforts to mass voting strength," Frankfurter noted. "Nor is this a case of boss-control, whether crudely or subtly exercised. Nor [even] a case of spontaneous efforts by citizens to influence votes or even continued efforts by a fraction of the electorate in support of good government." Rather, this was a case of public officials failing in their assigned constitutional tasks. Hence, although the Jaybirds' actions were not necessarily "proscribed by the Fifteenth amendment," the local officials' "role in the entire scheme to subvert the operation of the official primary" brought it "within reach of the law."

Only Justice Sherman Minton dissented, convinced that the Jaybirds were a purely private organization, and concerned that the Court was defining *state action* too broadly for constitutional safety. Minton's dissent did not mean that he endorsed the Jaybirds or their actions. "I am not concerned in the least as to what happens to the Jaybirds or their unworthy scheme," Minton wrote. "I am concerned about what this Court says is state action within the meaning of the Fifteenth Amendment to the Constitution. For, after all, this Court has power to redress a wrong under that Amendment only if the wrong is done by the State." The Jaybird Democratic Association, however, was a *private* organization. "It neither files, certifies, nor supplies anything for the primary or election. The winner of the poll in the Jaybird Association contest files in the Democratic primary, where he may and sometimes has received opposition, and successful opposition, in precinct contests for County Commissioner, Justice of the Peace and Constable. There is no rule of the Jaybird Association that requires the successful party in its poll to file in the Democratic primary or elsewhere. It is all individual, voluntary action. Neither the State nor the Democratic Party avails itself of the action of or cooperates in any manner with the Jaybird Association." True, the Jaybirds had been successful in getting their choices for candidate elected. Yet this was true "of concerted action by any group. In numbers there is strength. In organization there is effectiveness." How, then, did success translate into state action? The Jaybird Democratic Association was nothing more than a "pressure group," and "the courts do not normally pass upon [the constitutionality of] . . . pressure groups." Nor, Minton insisted, should they.

Although differing in their reasons for action, all the justices except Minton and Frankfurter agreed that the proper remedy in this case was for the Court to remand the case to the district court to "consider and determine what provisions are essential to afford Negro citizens of the County full protection from such future discriminatory election practices which deprive citizens of voting rights because of their color." Given that Judge Kennerly had already ordered the Jaybirds either to hold a race-neutral primary or to disband, the result was to end this last-gasp effort to retain the Texas AWP. When the Court in *Smith* ruled that all citizens have a right to a free and open ballot, notwithstanding issues of race, it meant it. The AWP was dead, and efforts to revive its ghost were *not* acceptable.

Those who had fought the AWP and its malign influence for so long welcomed its final collapse. Unfortunately, the AWP's demise was not an end to the fight for a meaningful vote for African Americans. The AWP had always been a means to an end. Its ultimate goal was to exclude blacks from *any* meaningful role in shaping public policy in the South. If the AWP really was forbidden, then Southern whites were determined to find some other form of exclusion and put it into effect. They were not about to allow blacks equal access to the polls, no matter what anyone — even the Supreme Court — declared.

Those seeking a replacement for the AWP lost no time in applying their ingenuity to the task. In Alabama, for instance, the legislature passed the 1946 Boswell Amendment to the state constitution limiting registration to those who, in the view of local registrars, "could 'understand and explain' any article of the federal constitution" — a requirement that local election officials made sure few blacks could meet. In 1948, a three-judge federal court concluded that the Boswell Amendment's "understand and explain" requirements did not provide "a reasonable standard" by which local registrars could properly administer their test. As written, the panel noted, the amendment gave a local election official "a naked and arbitrary power to give or withhold consent" according to that official's personal biases and had clearly been adopted for the sole "purpose of excluding Negro applicants for the franchise." The legislature's response was a constitutional amendment requiring the Alabama Supreme Court to create a uniform voter registration form the content of which, when written by that court, proved to be so complex and legalistic as to fulfill the same exclusionary result as the Boswell Amendment. Even more extreme was the 1957 gerrymandering of the municipal boundaries of Tuskegee, Alabama, to exclude all but four or five of the city's four hundred or so qualified black voters (but none of the whites) from city elections. Less drastic, but perhaps for this reason more effective, was a 1951 state law prohibiting "single-shot" voting in at-large county elections. In at-large elections, all the candidates run against one another, with the top vote getters filling the available seats. Single-shot voting occurs when members of a particular subgroup vote for only one candidate, giving up their ability to vote for others to ensure that their preferred candidate is one of the top vote getters. Under the 1951 law, any ballot on which the voter cast only one vote, not using up his or her available votes, was disqualified, making single-shot voting impossible and, thus, undermining the ability of blacks to elect even one candidate in an at-large election.

After Georgia's attempt to privatize the AWP failed, the state government focused its revised discriminatory efforts on undermining black voter registration. In 1949, the Georgia legislature enacted a "registration and purge" law. Under this statute, any voter who failed to vote at least once in a two-year period was automatically expunged from the voter rolls. Further, anyone reregistering following removal from the election lists (or registering for the first time) had either to pass the state's existing literacy test or to answer ten of thirty questions aimed at proving his or her "good character" and "understanding of the duties of citizenship." A 1958 statute increased the difficulty level of the questions while simultaneously expanding the number of required correct answers to twenty of thirty. The state statutes left enforcement of the literacy and good-character tests to the discretion of unsympathetic, and usually hostile, local election officials whose standards were so demanding that even educated blacks had trouble passing these tests; for illiterate blacks, they proved to be an almost insurmountable barrier. The unsurprising result was that few Georgia blacks could exercise their voting rights even fifteen years after the defeat of the AWP. In Terrell County, for instance, although 64 percent of the residents were black, only forty-eight blacks had registered to vote by 1958; by 1960, the number had grown only to fifty-three. Similar dismal registration numbers were found in Sumpter County as well: with a black plurality of 44 percent, only 8.2 percent of blacks were registered to vote in the early 1960s.

Mississippi likewise turned to local county registrars to limit black voting. The 1890 "Mississippi Plan" had kept blacks from the polls for over sixty years. Subsequent laws had added a "moral-character" test to the state's laundry list of effective exclusionary techniques. When the all-white primaries ended, these laws were still in force. Thus, local and state officials turned to the plan's most exclusionary component, the literacy test, to maintain white-only voting. As the historian Frank R. Parker describes in his *Black Votes Count*, under this rule, applicants seeking to register to vote "had to demonstrate their literacy by filling out in their own handwriting and without any assistance a long, complicated voter registration form asking detailed questions regarding occupation and business, residence, and criminal record." Applicants were also required to "copy any section of the Mississippi Constitution chosen by the registrar, write a correct interpretation of that section, and then explain in writing 'your understanding of the duties and obligations of citizenship under a constitutional form of government.'" Any mistake or error in filling out the form automatically disqualified the application. It was at this point that local officials stepped in, assuring white electoral dominance by selectively enforcing the literacy requirement. In fact, registrars routinely failed black applicants for such simple mistakes as not signing their name on the correct line of the form. When black voters overcame the barrier of the literacy test, registrars would refuse to credit black answers to the moral-character test. Often registrars would fail an applicant for misinterpreting a complicated passage of the state constitution — a passage that, as Parker notes, "they themselves could not interpret." And, as if such restrictive rules were not enough, local newspapers published the names of all those taking the registration test; intimidation, reprisals, and outright violence soon followed.

Renewed Southern efforts to maintain white electoral dominance spread like a shadow across the South. North Carolina centralized control over elections, established intricate procedures for voter registration, and granted extensive powers to local registrars to use these complex registration procedures to undermine black voting. South Carolina responded to *Elmore v. Rice* by adopting three measures aimed at diluting black voting strength: (1) extending the literacy test to party primaries; (2) adopting "full-slate" and "majority-vote" requirements for those same elections; and (3) shifting from district to at-large electoral systems in county elections. Texas placed its faith in a poll tax that, although only a small sum ($1.75), still was prohibitive for poor black laborers, for whom it was a day's wages. Virginia allowed a proportionally larger black vote in primaries and general elections than did other Southern states — but largely because it had faith that the existing system of poll taxes, "understanding" requirements, and literacy tests would limit the electoral impact of black voting. Louisiana used a constitutional "interpretation" test, along with a system by which any two registered voters could legally challenge the registration of another voter, to purge blacks from the voter rolls. Meanwhile, Arkansas gave up its attempt at a two-tiered primary system and trusted in informal violence as a deterrent to black voting.

Although such efforts to exclude black voting were not completely successful in stopping all black registration and/or voting, the results were still considerable. In 1940, only 3 percent of Southern blacks of voting age or older had been registered to vote — and, with the AWP, none were able to vote in the one election that had practical meaning. Following *Smith*, this situation began to change. By 1956, 25 percent of voting-age blacks were registered to vote; by 1964, this number increased to 43.3 percent across the South. In Texas, these percentages meant that, whereas in 1940 only about 30,000 Texas blacks were registered voters, by 1947 the number stood at 100,000— a more than threefold increase. By 1956, this number had increased to 214,000 registered black voters. Similar, if smaller, numbers could be found in other Southern states.

Raw numbers can be deceiving, however. Most registered black voters lived in the northern tier of border states or in Texas or Florida. In the Deep South, where most blacks lived, African American voter registration stood at only 22.5 percent as late as 1964, with Mississippi reporting the lowest percentage, 6.7 percent (although this was a notable increase from 1.98 percent a mere two years earlier). Worse yet, the application of such vote dilution techniques as purges of voting lists, at-large elections, and full-slate and majority-vote requirements — not to mention the ever-present threats of economic reprisal and physical violence against any black trying to vote — meant that, even in those areas where blacks made up a majority of the population, no black candidates were elected to office. Things got so bad that Margaret Price, vice chair of the Democratic National Committee, maintained in 1959 that, "for Negroes in some sections of the South, an attempt to exercise their right of franchise as Americans seemed a greater risk in 1958 than at any time since the outlawing of the white primary in 1944." In fact, it was exactly in those counties where blacks most outnumbered whites that black enfranchisement was at its lowest; the specter of black political power so terrified local whites that it spurred them to extraordinary efforts to keep blacks from the polls.

The AWP was dead. The victory was real. However, the fight for a racially balanced voting process — for a discrimination-free and open ballot — remained ongoing. And, although there would be victories in the fight against the newer, more intricate methods of vote denial — the overturning of the Boswell Amendment in 1948, the Supreme Court's ruling in *Terry v. Adams* (1953), and enactment of the Voting Rights Act of 1965 — as late as the mid-1960s, large numbers of Southern blacks still lacked an effective voice in shaping the South's political institutions and public policies.

Happily, this continuing battle would also achieve a successful conclusion. Although it took almost two decades following *Smith* before the South experienced what the legal sociologist Chandler Davidson and the political scientist Bernard Grofman have labeled the *Quiet Revolution* in Southern politics and life (the rise of black political power across the South), that revolution did happen. And the first step on this road to social and political revolution was the defeat of the Texas AWP.

"The *Smith v. Allwright* decision," writes the historian Darlene Clark Hine, author of the most complete history of the fight against the AWP, was a "watershed in the struggle for black rights. It signaled the beginning of the so-called Second Reconstruction and the modern civil rights movement." More to the point, it marked the beginning of the end of African American political exclusion in the South. "The political and social advances of blacks could not have occurred without the changes that came in the wake of the overthrow of the Democratic white primary." The results, as James O. Freedman, the former law clerk to Justice Thurgood Marshall, notes, "forever changed the profile of city halls, state capitols, and governors' mansions."

Ironically, it was the fact that *Smith* scared the white Southern leadership so much that it felt *forced* to intensify disenfranchisement efforts — to adopt and/or intensify a series of ever more intense, explicit forms of race-based vote denial to keep blacks from voting — that proved *Smith*'s greatest achievement. For, although the *immediate* impact was the continued denial of African American voting rights, the *long-term* effects of these blatant efforts to exclude blacks from the polls was to give civil rights leaders the ammunition that they needed to force the federal government into forcing change. And it would be these legal and legislative changes — most significantly, the passage of the Voting Rights Act of 1965 — that opened the door to power and acceptance for Southern blacks.

It was with this in mind that Thurgood Marshall observed in a 1977 interview that it was *Smith v. Allwright*, and not *Brown v. Board of Education*, that he deemed perhaps the most significant victory of his career. Granted, *Brown* was a ruling of clear historic significance, and Marshall took great pride in this hard-won victory. Still, it was *Smith* that opened the door to black voting and, in doing so, "changed the whole complexion of the South." As Marshall saw things, the vote was an essential first step to instigating any lasting change — political, economic, or social. What good were desegregated schools if the newly educated black population could not put its newly acquired education into action? This fact alone, Marshall argued in a 1957 article, made the victory in *Smith* "an important and distinct chapter in the story of the Negro's struggle for political equality."

It began as the dream of one African American dentist to take part in the simple act of voting, to join in the process by which we organize and control our public realm. Yet the fight to defeat the Texas AWP was always much more: it was a first step — a giant step — in the fifty-year struggle for African American civil rights. And its achievements and results reverberated across the civil rights spectrum. Although other victories provided momentum in the fight for equal rights, the fact that it was *Smith* — a voting rights case — that first served this function gave the drive for black civil rights extra impetus. As Marshall was noted to have said more than once by James Freedman: "Without the ballot, you have no citizenship, no status, no power in this country." Yet, with the ballot, the chance to gain power — and, with it, the possibility of forcing change — is always present. And the ability to force change was, and is, the essential ingredient in the fight for equitable civil rights.

# CHRONOLOGY

1866  Passage of the Thirteenth Amendment outlaws slavery and, by implication, grants full citizenship rights to African Americans, including the right to vote.

1868  Passage of the Fourteenth Amendment defines the nature of citizenship and provides for the protection of basic "privileges and immunities" of citizenship.

1870  Passage of the Fifteenth Amendment declares: "The right of citizens of the United States to vote shall not be denied or abridged by the United States or by any state on account of race, color, or previous condition of servitude."

1873  In an effort to disenfranchise black voters, Georgia passes a law permitting local election supervisors to close the registration rolls to new applicants *except* during those times when black farmers are too busy to register, such as planting or harvest.

1875  Alabama includes education requirements (literacy tests, understanding requirements) for voting.

1877  In a compromise worked out to settle the disputed presidential election of 1876, Northern Republicans agree to end their Reconstruction efforts in return for Southern Democrats' acceptance of Republican candidate Rutherford B. Hayes's victory. This compromise sets the stage for the eventual disenfranchisement of blacks by Southern states at the end of the century.

1882  South Carolina implements the Eight-Box Ballot Law. Under this rule, ballots for individual offices must be placed in separate ballot boxes. Put a ballot in the wrong box, and it will not be counted. The result is the effective disenfranchisement of illiterate South Carolina blacks.

1890  Mississippi implements the Mississippi Plan to disenfranchise blacks. The plan includes (1) a $2 poll tax payable before registration; (2) a literacy test in which voters must read, understand, or interpret any section of the state constitution to the satisfaction of a white (and usually hostile) election official; (3) long-term residency rules demanding two years' domicile within the state and one year's within the voting district; and (4) permanent disenfranchisement for crimes felt most likely to be committed by blacks. States across the South soon adopt similar comprehensive disenfranchisement plans.

1892    The rise of Populism threatens Democratic control of Texas state government.

1895    In an effort to disenfranchise black voters, South Carolina requires all potential voters to read and/or explain any section of the state constitution provided by the local voting registrar prior to being allowed to register to vote.

1896–    All-white primaries are adopted in states across the South.
1915

1902    Texas adopts poll taxes for voting.

1903    The Terrell Election Law implements an all-white Democratic primary in Texas.

1905    Texas updates and expands the reach of its all-white primary (AWP) laws.

1909    The National Association for the Advancement of Colored People (NAACP) forms with the primary objective of enlarging the ongoing struggle for African American civil and political liberty.

1917    NAACP President Moorfield Storey files an *amicus curiae* (lit. "friend of the court," i.e., interested third party) brief on behalf of the association in the Supreme Court case *Guinn v. United States* (overturning the constitutionality of Oklahoma's grandfather statute, which permitted illiterate whites, but not blacks, to vote).

1921    The U.S. Supreme Court holds in *Newberry v. United States* that primary elections are *not* part of the election process regulated by the civil rights amendments. Texas blacks unsuccessfully file suit in state court challenging the AWP in *Love v. Griffith*. A similar outcome follows in the federal case *Chandler v. Neff.*

1923    The Texas legislature revises the state primary law in order expressly to prohibit *as a matter of state law* black voting in the Democratic primaries.

1924    At the request of El Paso's NAACP local president, L. W. Washington, Dr. Lawrence A. Nixon challenges the state's AWP laws.

1927    The Supreme Court in *Nixon v. Herndon* holds Texas's 1923 voting-rights law imposing an AWP to be an unconstitutional violation of the Fourteenth Amendment. Unfortunately, as this opinion deals only with the explicit prohibition of black voting by the legislature, the Court's ruling leaves a loophole that allows the state to continue the AWP by devolving this power back to the Democratic Party — which the state quickly does by legislative enactment.

1928    In *Grigsby v. Harris*, U.S. District Judge Joseph C. Hutcheson of the Southern District of Texas ignores the clear intent of the Supreme Court's ruling in *Nixon v. Herndon* and sustains the 1927 revision of the Texas election laws as constitutional.

1932    In *Nixon v. Condon*, the Supreme Court rules that the Texas Democratic Party is *not* a simple voluntary association — at least as regards primary elections. Rather, the party is an agent of the state, deriving its authority directly from a "grant of power" from the state, and, as such, its imposition of an AWP is a form of prohibited "state action" under the Fourteenth Amendment. Soon after, in *White v. County Democratic Executive Committee of Harris County*, Thomas Kennerly, the new district judge of the Southern District of Texas, ignores the Supreme Court ruling and, once again, upholds the Texas AWP as constitutional.

1935    The Supreme Court in *Grovey v. Townsend* accepts the Texas Democratic Party convention's updated rules barring blacks from the Democratic primary. This permits the practice of all-white primaries to continue for another twelve years. Charles Hamilton Houston becomes the NAACP special counsel charged with organizing and leading the legal fight against segregation and other forms of race-based discrimination.

1936    Houston names his former student, Thurgood Marshall, as his assistant.

1940    Thurgood Marshall takes over as NAACP special counsel and helps organize the Legal Defense and Education Fund (LDF) as a separately funded legal arm of the NAACP. The LDF files suit in the case *Hasgett v. Werner*, attacking the Texas AWP, but loses in the Southern District Court of Texas.

1941    The Supreme Court rules in *United States v. Classic* that Article 1, Section 4, of the U.S. Constitution gives Congress the power to regulate primary elections "where the primary is by law made an integral part of the election machinery." Soon after, Marshall files suit in the Southern District Court of Texas on behalf of Dr. Lonnie Smith, challenging the Texas AWP as incompatible with the Supreme Court's ruling in *Classic*.

1942    *Smith v. Allwright* is argued before the Southern District Court
        of Texas, where Judge Thomas Kennerly rules in favor of the
        state and the constitutionality of the AWP. Soon after, the Fifth
        Circuit Court of Appeals upholds Judge Kennerly's ruling.

1944    The Supreme Court invalidates the AWP in Texas (and, by
        implication, across the South) in *Smith v. Allwright*. The Court
        holds that, in the light of *United States v. Classic*'s holding that
        primary elections do come under the Fifteenth Amendment's
        purview, the Texas Democratic Party's control of the state's
        primary system is evidence that it operates as an "agency of the
        state" — even with the vote by the party's full membership that it
        does not want black members — and, hence, is prohibited by the
        Constitution. Days later, in an effort to avoid the Court's *Smith*
        ruling, South Carolina revises its state laws to remove *any*
        mention of primary elections.

1945    In *King v. Chapman*, U.S. District Judge T. Hoyt Davis rules
        that the High Court's invalidation of Texas's AWP applies
        to Georgia. The Fifth Circuit later upholds this reading of
        the case.

1947    U.S. District Judge J. Waties Waring declares South Carolina's
        attempt to rewrite its election laws in order to "completely
        renounce control of political parties and [the] primaries held
        there under" unconstitutional in *Elmore v. Rice*.

1948    Judge Waring, in *Brown v. Baskin*, negates efforts by South
        Carolina Democrats to undermine his decision in *Elmore v. Rice*
        by "privatizing" the primary process (by removing all mention of
        the primary from state law).

1949    The Fourth Circuit Court of Appeals upholds Judge Waring's
        ruling in *Brown v. Baskin*.

1950    Southern District of Texas Judge Thomas Kennerly holds against
        the segregated Jaybird Democratic Association (a purportedly
        self-governing voluntary private club that puts forth a slate of
        candidates who "nearly always" run unopposed in the
        Democratic primaries) in *Terry v. Adams*.

1952    The Fifth Circuit Court of Appeals reverses the district court
        ruling in *Terry v. Adams*, holding: "There was no constitutional
        or congressional bar to the admitted discriminatory exclusion of
        Negroes because Jaybird's primaries were not to any extent state
        controlled."

1953    The Supreme Court reverses the Fifth Circuit in *Terry v. Adams*, supporting instead the district court's ruling declaring the Jaybird primary an impermissible racial discrimination.

1957    Passage of the Civil Rights Act of 1957 provides some small legislative support for black voting rights.

1960    Passage of the Civil Rights Act of 1960 adds still more legislative support for black voting rights.

1965    Passage of the Voting Rights Act of 1965 provides extensive federal support for defending and enhancing black voting rights in the South.

# RELEVANT CASES

*Adams v. Terry*, 193 F.2d 600 (1952)
*Baker v. Carr*, 369 U.S. 186 (1962)
*Baskin v. Brown*, 174 F.2d 391 (1949)
*Bell v. Hill*, 74 S.W.2d 113 (1934)
*Breedlove v. Suttles*, 302 U.S. 277 (1937)
*Brown v. Baskin*, 78 F. Supp. 933 (1948)
*Brown v. Board of Education*, 337 U.S. 483 (1954)
*Brown v. Board of Education II*, 349 U.S. 294 (1955)
*Buchanan v. Warley*, 245 U.S. 60 (1917)
*Chandler v. Neff*, 298 F. 515 (1924)
*Corrigan v. Buckley*, 271 U.S. 323 (1926)
*Dred Scott v. Sanford*, 60 U.S. 393 (1856)
*Elmore v. Rice*, 72 F. Supp. 516 (1947)
*Grigsby v. Harris*, 772 So. 2d 1243 (1928)
*Grovey v. Townsend*, 295 U.S. 45 (1935)
*Guinn v. United States*, 228 F. 103 (1915)
*Hasgett v. Werner*, Civil Action 449, Houston Division, SD of Texas (1941)
*King v. Chapman*, 62 F. Supp. 639 (1945)
*Love v. Griffith*, 236 S.W. 239 (1921)
*Love v. Griffith*, 266 U.S. 32 (1924)
*Love v. Wilcox*, 119 Tex. 256 (1930)
*Moore v. Dempsey*, 261 U.S. 86 (1923)
*Morgan v. Virginia*, 328 U.S. 373 (1946)
*Newberry v. United States*, 256 U.S. 232 (1921)
*Nixon v. Condon*, 286 U.S. 73 (1932)
*Nixon v. Herndon*, 273 U.S. 536 (1927)
*Richardson v. Executive Committee of the Democratic Party for the City of Houston*,
    Civil Action 20, Houston Division, SD of Texas (1938)
*Shelly v. Kraemer*, 334 U.S. 1 (1948)
*Slaughterhouse Cases*, 16 Wall. 36 (1873)
*Smith v. Allwright*, Civil Action 645, Houston Division, SD of Texas (1942)
*Smith v. Allwright*, 131 F.2d 593 (1942)
*Smith v. Allwright*, 321 U.S. 649 (1944)
*Sweatt v. Painter*, 339 U.S. 626 (1950)
*Terry v. Adams*, 90 F. Supp. 595 (1950)
*Terry v. Adams*, 345 U.S. 461 (1953)
*United States v. Classic*, 313 U.S. 299 (1941)
*United States v. Cruikshank*, 92 U.S. 542 (1876)

*United States v. Reese*, 92 U.S. 214 (1876)

*White v. County Democratic Executive Committee of Harris County*, 60 F.2d 973 (1932)

*White v. Lubbock*, 30 S.W.2d 722 (1930)

# BIBLIOGRAPHIC ESSAY

As with most of the other volumes in the Landmark Law Cases and American Society series, *The Battle for the Black Ballot* is a synthetic work built on the twin foundations of primary research and existing secondary sources. Happily, both types of sources are available in large numbers. All quotes and details are drawn from these sources, primary and secondary, which are listed below. Also included here are additional sources useful to those wishing to dig deeper into the history of the all-white primary (AWP), the fight of the National Association for the Advancement of Colored People (NAACP) for equal rights, and/or voting-rights history in general.

Many primary source materials on *Smith v. Allwright* and other associated white-primary cases can be found in published form. The case decisions themselves are published in the *Federal Supplement* (district court rulings), the *Federal Reporter* (circuit court rulings), and the *United States Reports* (Supreme Court rulings). State cases are available in the *Southwestern Reporter.* Citations to these cases are given in the list of relevant cases. Supreme Court briefs in *Smith* are reprinted in Philip Kurland and Gerhard Casper, eds., *Landmark Briefs and Arguments of the Supreme Court of the United States* (Washington, D.C.: University Publications of America, 1975), vol. 41. Conference notes can be found in Del Dickson, ed., *The Supreme Court in Conference, 1940–1985* (Oxford: Oxford University Press, 2001).

Additional primary materials on these cases are available at the National Archives Branch in Fort Worth, Texas. This includes files from all federal district and circuit court cases filed in Texas. Most of these files will include, not only copies of the Court's rulings, but also briefs and other pleadings presented by the litigants. Transcripts of court proceedings are, in some cases (e.g., *Smith*), also available.

Supreme Court justices' papers are another useful source of information. Often they will include multiple drafts of opinions and/or internal memorandums useful to understanding the internal workings of the Court as it struggled with these matters. In particular, the papers of Justice Felix Frankfurter (archived at Harvard University and available on microfilm from the University Publications of America) and Justice Tom Clark (archived at the Rare Book and Special Collections, Tarlton Law Library, University of Texas at Austin) were of use in researching this book. Other important collections include the Thurgood Marshall Papers, on file in the Manuscript Division of the Library of Congress, and the Stanley Reed Papers, found at the Special Collections and Archives, King Library, University of Kentucky.

The National Association for the Advancement of Colored People's Papers are still another key resource to understanding the evolution of the fight against the AWP. The correspondence and memorandums found within these files provide a window into both the litigation process as a whole and the conflicting objectives of the national office and the local Texas branches in shaping this process. They are also the source of most of the letters and memorandums quoted in this book. Archived in the Manuscripts Division of the Library of Congress, they are available on microfilm from the University Publications of America under the title *Papers of the NAACP*, pt. 4, *The Voting Rights Campaign, 1916–1950*.

The vast majority of Thurgood Marshall's speeches and writings — in addition to a full transcript of Marshall's 1977 oral history interview for the Columbia University Oral History Research Office — have been reprinted in Mark V. Tushnet, *Thurgood Marshall: His Speeches, Writings, Arguments, Opinions, and Reminiscences* (Chicago: Lawrence Hill, 2001).

Finally, newspapers provide a useful source of information and commentary on the events surrounding the fight against the AWP. Especially helpful in this regard is the *Houston Informer*, which provides the fullest contemporary coverage of the fight against the Texas AWP. All the papers quoted in the book are available via microfilm and/or in archived collections. Most of the quoted newspaper passages can also be found quoted in the books, articles, and dissertations listed below.

In addition to these primary materials, a large number of secondary books and articles are available that explore aspects of the fight against the AWP. Most useful in this regard, and the starting place for anyone wishing to delve deeper into this story, is Darlene Clark Hine, *Black Victory: The Rise and Fall of the White Primary in Texas* (Millwood, N.Y.: KTO, 1979). Other crucial sources of information are Steven F. Lawson, *Black Ballots: Voting Rights in the South, 1944–1969* (1976; Lanham, Md.: Lexington, 1999), esp. chap. 2, "The Rise and Fall of the White Primary"; Mark V. Tushnet, *Making Civil Rights Law: Thurgood Marshall and the Supreme Court, 1936–1961* (Oxford: Oxford University Press, 1994), esp. chap. 7, " 'Interference with the Effective Choice of the Voters': Challenging the White Primary"; Robert V. Haynes, "Black Houstonians and the White Democratic Primary, 1920–1945," in *Black Dixie: Afro-Texan History and Culture in Houston*, ed. Howard Beeth and Cary D. Wintz (College Station: Texas A&M University Press, 1992), 192–210; Conrey Bryson, *Dr. Lawrence A. Nixon and the White Primary*, rev. ed. (1974; El Paso: Texas Western, 1992); Alan Robert Burch, "Charles Hamilton Houston, the Texas White Primary, and Centralization of the NAACP's Litigation Strategy," *Thurgood Marshall Law Review* 21 (fall 1995): 95–153; Darlene Clark Hine, "Blacks and the Destruction of the Democratic White Primary, 1935–1944," *Journal of Negro History* 62 (January 1997): 43–59; Thurgood Marshall, "The Rise and Collapse of the 'White Democratic Primary,' " *Journal of Negro Education* 26 (summer 1957): 249–54; Robert E. Cushman, "The

Texas 'White Primary' Case — *Smith v. Allwright*," *Cornell Law Quarterly* 30 (September 1944): 66–76; Randal W. Bland, "Thurgood Marshall and the Texas White Primary," *Texas Observer*, February 26, 1993, 21; Robert Wendell Hainsworth, "The Negro and the Texas Primaries," *Journal of Negro History* 18 (October 1933): 426–50; Leo Alilunas, "The Rise of the 'White Primary' Movement as a Means of Barring the Negro from the Polls," *Journal of Negro History* 25 (April 1940): 161–72; O. Douglass Weeks, "The White Primary: 1944–1948," *American Political Science Review* 42 (June 1948): 500–510; Fred Folsom, "Federal Elections and the 'White Primary,'" *Columbia Law Review* 43 (November–December 1943): 1026–1935; James O. Freedman, "The Tyrrell Williams Memorial Lecture: Thurgood Marshall: Man of Character," *Washington University Law Quarterly* 72 (1994): 1487–1505.

For more general background to this case, see Charles L. Zelden, *Justice Lies in the District: The United States District Court, Southern District of Texas, 1902–1960* (College Station: Texas A&M University Press, 1993); Donald S. Strong, "The Rise of Negro Voting in Texas," *American Political Science Review* 42 (June 1948): 510–22; Alpheus Thomas Mason, *The Supreme Court from Taft to Warren*, rev. and enlarged ed. (Baton Rouge: Louisiana State University Press, 1968); Leo Alilunas, "A Study of Judicial Cases Which Have Developed as the Result of 'White Primary' Laws," *Journal of Negro History* 25 (April 1940): 172–80; Louise Overacker, "The Negro's Struggle for Participation in Primary Elections," *Journal of Negro History* 30 (January 1945): 54–61; J. Woodford Howard Jr., *Mr. Justice Murphy: A Political Biography* (Princeton, N.J.: Princeton University Press, 1968); James F. Simon, *The Antagonists: Hugo Black, Felix Frankfurter, and Civil Liberties in Modern America* (New York: Simon & Schuster, 1989); Mark Silverstein, *Constitutional Faiths: Felix Frankfurter, Hugo Black, and the Process of Judicial Decision Making* (Ithaca, N.Y.: Cornell University Press, 1984); Howard Ball, *A Defiant Life: Thurgood Marshall and the Persistence of Racism in America* (New York: Crown, 1998); Carl T. Rowan, *Dream Makers, Dream Breakers: The World of Justice Thurgood Marshall* (Boston: Little, Brown, 1993); Randall W. Bland, *Private Pressure on Public Law: The Legal Career of Justice Thurgood Marshall* (Port Washington, N.Y.: Kennikat, 1973); Juan Williams, *Thurgood Marshall: American Revolutionary* (New York: Times Books, 1998); Gerald T. Dunne, *Hugo Black and the Judicial Revolution* (New York: Simon & Schuster, 1977).

For a discussion of the cases that followed *Smith v. Allwright*, see Michael J. Klarman, "The White Primary Rulings: A Case Study in the Consequences of Supreme Court Decision Making," *Florida State University Law Review* 29 (fall 2001): 55–107; Pauline Yelderman, *The Jaybird Democratic Association of Fort Bend County: A White Man's Union* (Waco, Tex.: Texian, 1979); C. Calvin Smith, "The Politics of Evasion: Arkansas' Reaction to *Smith v. Allwright*, 1944," *Journal of Negro History* 67 (spring 1982): 40–51; Charles D. Farris,

"The Re-Enfranchisement of Negroes in Florida," *Journal of Negro History* 39 (October 1954): 259–83; David W. Southern, "Beyond Jim Crow Liberalism: Judge Waring's Fight against Segregation in South Carolina, 1942–52," *Journal of Negro History* 66 (autumn 1981): 209–27; Tinsley E. Yarbrough, *A Passion for Justice: J. Waties Waring and Civil Rights* (Oxford: Oxford University Press, 1987); Harry Holloway, "The Negro and the Vote: The Case of Texas," *Journal of Politics* 3 (August 1961): 526–56; Margaret Price, *The Negro and the Ballot in the South* (Atlanta: Southern Regional Council, 1959).

A number of books, articles, and doctoral dissertations provide useful background information on the Texas context. These include Alwyn Barr, *Black Texans: A History of Negroes in Texas, 1528–1971* (Austin, Tex.: Pemberton, 1973); Alwyn Barr, *Reconstruction to Reform: Texas Politics, 1876–1906* (Austin: University of Texas Press, 1971); Lawrence D. Rice, *The Negro in Texas, 1874–1900* (Baton Rouge: Louisiana State University Press, 1971); James M. SoRelle, "The Darker Side of 'Heaven': The Black Community in Houston, Texas, 1917–1945" (Ph.D. diss., Kent State University, 1980); William J. Brophy, "The Black Texan, 1900–1950: A Quantitative History" (Ph.D. diss., Vanderbilt University, 1974); Neil Gary Sapper, "A Survey of the History of the Black People of Texas, 1930-1954" (Ph.D. diss., Texas Tech University, 1972); Chandler Davidson, "Negro Politics and the Rise of the Civil Rights Movement in Houston, Texas" (Ph.D. diss., Princeton University, 1968); Chandler Davidson, *Race and Class in Texas Politics* (Princeton, N.J.: Princeton University Press, 1990); David Montejano, *Anglos and Mexicans in the Making of Texas, 1836–1986* (Austin: University of Texas Press, 1987); Robert A. Calvert and Arnoldo De Leon, *The History of Texas* (Arlington Heights, Ill.: Harlan Davidson, 1990); Judith Kaaz Doyle, "Maury Maverick and Racial Politics in San Antonio, Texas, 1938–1941," *Journal of Southern History* 53 (May 1987): 194–224; Charles Kincheloe Chamberlain, "Alexander Watkins Terrell, Citizen, Statesman" (Ph.D. diss., University of Texas, 1956).

On the impact of Reconstruction on the South, see Harold M. Hyman and William M. Wiecek, *Equal Justice under Law: Constitutional Development, 1835–1875* (New York: Harper & Row, 1982); Eric Foner, *Reconstruction: America's Unfinished Revolution, 1863–1877* (New York: Harper & Row, 1988); Harold M. Hyman, *A More Perfect Union: The Impact of the Civil War and Reconstruction on the Constitution* (New York: Knopf, 1973); Stanley L. Kutler, *Judicial Power and Reconstruction Politics* (Chicago: University of Chicago Press, 1968).

On the rise of African American disenfranchisement at the turn of the century, see Michael Perman, *Struggle for Mastery: Disfranchisement in the South, 1888–1908* (Chapel Hill: University of North Carolina Press, 2001); J. Morgan Kousser, *The Shaping of Southern Politics: Suffrage Restriction and the Establishment of the One-Party South, 1880–1910* (New Haven, Conn.: Yale University Press, 1974); V. O. Key, *Southern Politics in State and Nation* (New York: Knopf,

1949); C. Vann Woodward, *The Strange Career of Jim Crow*, rev. 2d ed. (Oxford: Oxford University Press, 1966); C. Vann Woodward, *Origins of the New South, 1877–1913* (1951; Baton Rouge: Louisiana State University Press, 1971); Edward L. Ayers, *The Promise of the New South: Life after Reconstruction* (Oxford: Oxford University Press, 1992); V. O. Key Jr., *Southern Politics in State and Union* (New York: Knopf, 1949); Alfred Holt Stone, *Studies in the American Race Problem* (New York: Doubleday, Page, 1908).

On the Populists, the Progressives, and other reform movements and their impact on African American voting, see Gregg Cantrell and D. Scott Barton, "Texas Populists and the Failure of Biracial Politics," *Journal of Southern History* 55 (November 1989): 659–92; Lawrence C. Goodwyn, "Populist Dreams and Negro Rights: East Texas as a Case Study," *American Historical Review* 76 (December 1971): 1435–56; Forrest G. Wood, "On Revising Reconstruction History, Negro Suffrage, White Disenfranchisement, and Common Sense," *Journal of Negro History* 51 (April 1966): 98–113; Evan Anders, *Boss Rule in South Texas: The Progressive Era* (Austin: University of Texas Press, 1982); Louis L. Gould, *Progressives and Prohibitionists: Texas Democrats in the Wilson Era* (Austin: University of Texas Press, 1973); Dewey W. Grantham, *Southern Progressivism: The Reconciliation of Progress and Tradition* (Knoxville: University of Tennessee Press, 1983); Worth Robert Miller, "Building a Progressive Coalition in Texas: The Populist–Reform Democrat Rapprochement, 1900–1907," *Journal of Southern History* 52 (May 1986): 163–82; Jack Abramowitz, "The Negro in the Populist Movement," *Journal of Negro History* 38 (July 1953): 257–89.

Background on the NAACP and its internal workings as it fought the AWP can be found in Michael Lowery Gillette, "The NAACP in Texas, 1937–1957" (Ph.D. diss., University of Texas at Austin, 1984); Burch, "Charles Hamilton Houston" (see above); Tushnet, *Making Civil Rights Law* (see above); Roger A. Fairfax Jr., "A Tribute to Charles Hamilton Houston: Wielding the Double-Edged Sword: Charles Hamilton Houston and Judicial Activism in the Age of Legal Realism," *Harvard Blackletter Journal* 14 (spring 1988): 17–44; August Meier and Elliott Rudwick, "Attorneys Black and White: A Case Study of Race Relations within the NAACP," *Journal of American History* 62 (March 1976): 913–46; Merline Pitre, *In Struggle against Jim Crow: Lulu B. White and the NAACP, 1900–1957* (College Station: Texas A&M University Press, 1999); U. W. Clemon and Bryan K. Fair, "Making Bricks without Straw: The NAACP Legal Defense Fund and the Development of Civil Rights Law in Alabama, 1940–1980," *Alabama Law Review* 52 (summer 2001): 1121–52.

For more general information on voting rights and race-based vote denial, see Charles L. Zelden, *Voting Rights on Trial* (Santa Barbara, Calif.: ABC-Clio, 2002); Alexander Keyssar, *The Right to Vote: The Contested History of Democracy in the United States* (New York: Basic, 2000); Francis Fox Piven and Richard Cloward, *Why Americans Don't Vote* (New York: Pantheon, 1988); Chandler Davidson and Bernard Grofman, eds., *Quiet Revolution in the South: The Impact of the Voting Rights Act, 1965–1990* (Princeton, N.J.: Princeton University Press, 1994); Eric Foner, "From Slavery to Citizenship: Blacks and the Right to Vote," in *Voting and the Spirit of American Democracy*, ed. Donald W. Rogers (1990; Urbana: University of Illinois Press, 1992), 55–65; Frank R. Parker, *Black Votes Count: Political Empowerment in Mississippi after 1965* (Chapel Hill: University of North Carolina Press, 1990), esp. chaps. 1–2.

Other general sources used in writing this book include Edmund S. Morgan, *American Slavery, American Freedom: The Ordeal of Colonial Virginia* (New York: Norton, 1975); Alexander Hamilton, James Madison, and John Jay, *The Federalist Papers* (New York: Mentor, 1961); Edward Pessen, *Jacksonian America: Society, Personality, and Politics* (1969; Urbana: University of Illinois Press, 1985); Dan T. Carter, *When the War Was Over: The Failure of Self-Reconstruction in the South, 1865–1867* (Baton Rouge: Louisiana State University Press, 1985); Foner, *Reconstruction* (see above); Robert M. Goldman, *Reconstruction and Black Suffrage: Losing the Vote in "Reese" and "Cruikshank"* (Lawrence: University Press of Kansas, 2001); Gavin Wright, *Old South, New South: Revolutions in the Southern Economy since the Civil War* (New York: Basic, 1986); Mark V. Tushnet, *The NAACP's Legal Strategy against Segregated Education, 1925–1950* (Chapel Hill: University of North Carolina Press, 1987); Raymond Wolters, *The Burden of Brown: Thirty Years of School Desegregation* (Knoxville: University of Tennessee Press, 1984); Richard Kluger, *Simple Justice* (New York: Vintage, 1975).

Marc Galanter's theoretical breakdown of the litigation process can be found in Marc Galanter, "Why the 'Haves' Come Out Ahead: Speculations on the Limits of Legal Change," *Law and Society Review* 9 (fall 1974): 95–160.

Justice Sandra Day O'Connor's comments on the workings of the Supreme Court can be found in the May 1988 PBS/WETA-TV video *This Honorable Court*, pt. 2, *Inside the Marble Temple* (available through the Greater Washington Educational Telecommunications Association, Washington, D.C.).

# INDEX

*Adams v. Terry*, 122–23
African Americans
   and black elected officials, 13
   end of Reconstruction, effects on
      voting of, 14–15
   lawyers as leaders in fight for civil
      rights, 72, 74
   numbers of registered voters, 17,
      109, 130–31
   population in South, 9
   and race-based vote exclusions, 6,
      15–16, 60, 93, 101
   response to AWP, 45
   and segregation, 7
   as swing voters in close elections,
      10, 37–38
   and threats of violence, 7
   and use of courts to fight
      segregation and discrimination,
      51–52
   and voting, 3, 10, 11, 13, 37–38,
      79, 97, 99, 130; in Democratic
      primaries, 109, 130
Alabama, State of, 14–15
   and Boswell Amendment, 127, 131
   disenfranchisement following
      *Smith v. Allwright*, 127–28
   impact of disenfranchisement on
      African American voting in, 18
   number of African American
      voters prior to 1900, 17
   and racially biased limits on voter
      registration, 16
   and vote denial, 18, 133
All-white primary (AWP), vii, 43,
   56, 61, 62–63, 65, 74, 75, 77,
   92, 94, 95, 109, 132, 134–36
   adoption of: by Southern states,
      2, 19, 20; by Texas counties in

      nineteenth century, 39; by
      Texas in 1903, 40–42
   argued unconstitutional, 62, 92,
      94–95, 97, 101–3
   declared unconstitutional, 63,
      101, 103–8
   defeat of, 3, 121
   definition, 20
   following ruling in *Smith v.*
      *Allwright*, 109–32
   link to poll tax, 37–39
   opposition to by Supreme Court
      in *Smith v. Allwright*, 100
   reasons adopted in Texas, 38, 51
   and *United States v. Classic*, 81–83
Allwright, S. E., 68
American Civil Liberties Union, 92
Arkansas, State of
   Democratic Party in, 114
   opposition to ruling in *Smith v.*
      *Allwright*, 114, 130
Ashe, Judge Charles, 52–53
Atkins, J. Alston, 59, 61–66,
   accepts NAACP litigation
      strategy, 75
   debate with NAACP over
      litigation strategy, 69, 71, 95
   objections to NAACP, 66

*Baker v. Carr*, viii
*Bell v. Hill*, 65, 67, 95, 96, 99, 104
Bexar County Election Board, 53
Biddle, Francis, 93
Black, Justice Hugo, 100, 123–24
Blackburn, John H., 79
Black Codes, 12
Black Texans
   and NAACP's litigation strategy,
      50

Black Texans, *continued*
    as "one shotters," 50
    and opposition to AWP, 49
    and relations with NAACP's
        national office, 48–49
Booker, C. A., 65
*Breedlove v. Suttles*, 47
*Brown v. Baskin*, 119, 136
*Brown v. Board of Education*, viii, 3,
    132
Bryan, William Jennings, 32
Bryant, Judge Randolph, 65
*Buchanan v. Warley*, 46
Burton, Justice Harold H., 123

Cardozo, Justice Benjamin N.,
    62–63, 64
Chandler, Hurley C., 53–54, 55
*Chandler v. Neff*, 53–54, 134
*Chicago Defender*, 109
Civil War, 10–11, 22, 23
Clark, George, 31
Clark, Justice Tom C., 124
Cobb, James A., 56
Colored Farmers' Alliance of
    Texas, 29
Condon, James, 58
*Corrigan v. Buckley*, 46
Courts as instrument of social and
    political change, 69
Culberson, Charles A., 31–32, 33

*Dallas Times Herald*, 110
Daniels, Josephus, 38
Davis, Judge T. Hoyt, 113, 115–16,
    136
Democratic Party
    as agent of the state in Texas,
        62–63, 79–80, 82–84, 86–88,
        96–97, 100, 104, 106
    attack on Populist threat,
        31–33

county Democratic Party boards,
    41
effects of victory in *Smith v.
    Allwright* on, 3
effects of victory over Populism
    on, 33–42
    in Florida, 113
    and legislative adoption of AWP
        in 1923, 44, 51
    national, 66
National Committee, 130
opposition to ruling in *Smith v.
    Allwright*, 111
primary elections, 2, 21; after
    ruling in *Smith v. Allwright*,
    109; in Texas, 37–44, 50–51,
    55, 66–67, 68, 80, 82–83, 86,
    93, 96, 99, 100–101, 103–8
    as a private agency, 58, 61, 68, 75,
        80, 85, 96, 99
    public vs. private nature of, 60,
        81, 104
    reaction to *Nixon v. Condon*, 59
    reaction to *Nixon v. Herndon*, 57
    in South Carolina, 116–21
    in Texas, 1, 28, 29, 68–69, 79, 89,
        95–97, 121–27
    Texas State Executive
        Committee, 41, 61
    *see also under* Texas, State of
Department of Justice, 81, 92–93
DeWalt, Owen, 57–58
Disenfranchisement
    after defeat of AWP, 127–32
    and at-large voting, 15, 128,
        129
    and AWP, 19, 33–44, 45, 50–51,
        93, 97, 101, 127
    and felony exclusions, 16, 18, 19,
        20, 133
    following Reconstruction, 14–15
    following World War One, 42

as foundation to Jim Crow segregation, 6
and "grandfather" clauses, 18
and intimidation, 129
and literacy tests, 2, 16, 17, 19, 20, 128, 129, 133–34
and "majority-vote" and "full-slate" requirements, 129–30
and "moral-character" tests, 129
and poll taxes, 2, 16, 19, 20, 36, 38, 45, 47, 109, 129–30, 133–34
presented as electoral reform, 34–37
and racial gerrymandering, 2, 15, 47, 127
and "registration and purge" laws, 128, 129, 130
and residency requirements, 18, 133
as a response to defeat of Populists, 33–44
and "single-shot" voting requirements, 128
and "understanding" requirements, 2, 20, 128, 129–30, 133–34
unexpected consequences in Texas of, 36–38
Douglas, Justice William O., 100, 123
*Dred Scott v. Sanford*, 68
Durham, W. J., 77, 93

Eastland, Senator James O., 110
*Elmore v. Rice*, 117–18, 129, 136
Eugene, C. S., 65
Evans, R. D., 58, 71

Fahy, Charles, 93
Farmers' Alliance, 27–29

Fifteenth Amendment, 3–4, 12, 20, 40, 52–53, 55, 57, 60, 68, 79–80, 93, 105–6, 116, 122, 123–24, 126, 133
and regulation of primary elections, 61–62, 76
and state-action requirement, 43, 60–61, 103
First Amendment, 99
Florida, State of
and 2000 presidential election, 5
attempt to privatize primaries, 113
and Democratic state committee, 113
opposition to ruling in *Smith v. Allwright*, 112, 113–14, 130
Folsom, Fred, 93
Fort Bend County, Texas
and Jaybird Democratic Association, 39, 115, 121–27
and use of "preprimaries," 115, 121–27
and "Woodpeckers" vs. "Jaybirds" conflicts, 38
*Fort Worth Star-Telegram*, 110
"Four Freedoms," 97
Fourteenth Amendment, vii, 3–4, 12, 20, 46, 52, 53, 55, 56–57, 63, 68, 79, 93, 106, 116, 122, 133, 135
equal protection clause, 57, 60, 66
limits of reach, 14
and regulation of primary elections, 62, 66, 76
and state-action requirement, 14, 43, 57, 60–61, 103
Franchise, 5–6, 94
African American, 10, 12–13
importance of for African American civil rights, 12

and poll taxes, 36, 38, 115; effects of on voting, 36–37
and Populists, 28–29
and reform Democrats, 28, 40
and south Texas political bosses, 35–37, 41
and state Democratic convention, 63
and state Democratic Executive Committee, 41, 58, 61, 98
and tenant farming (share-cropping), 23–25, 27, 29, 37
and Terrell Election Law, 40–42, 50, 134
unexpected consequences of disenfranchisement in, 37–38
and vote denial, 18, 41
and voting after *Smith v. Allwright*, 109, 121–27
and "white primary clubs," 38–39, 115
Texas Supreme Court, 43, 54, 60, 67, 96, 99
Thirteenth Amendment, 11, 133
Tobin, John, 43
Townsend, Albert, 66

United States Circuit Court for the Fifth Circuit, 3, 64, 80, 86–88, 115, 122–23, 136–37
United States Circuit Court for the Fourth Circuit, 118, 120, 136
United States District Court for the Eastern District of Louisiana, 81
United States District Court for the Northern District of Texas, 3, 65
United States District Court for the Southern District of Texas, 55, 64, 67, 75, 79, 84–86, 121–22, 135–36

United States District Court for the Western District of Texas, 53, 55, 58
United States district courts, 64
United States Supreme Court, vii, 3, 58, 79
and acceptance of literacy tests and racial gerrymandering, 47
changes in membership, 77
in conference, 91, 100–102
and *Grovey v. Townsend*, 65–67
judicial function, 89
and *Newberry v. United States* ruling, 43
and *Nixon v. Herndon*, 56–57
opposition to AWP in *Smith v. Allwright*, 100
and *Smith v. Allwright*, 4, 89–108
and *Terry v. Adams*, 123–27
and *United States v. Classic*, 81–83
*United States v. Classic*, 80–83, 85, 87, 89–90, 92–97, 99–101, 103–4, 106, 117, 135–36
*United States v. Cruikshank*, 14
*United States v. Reese*, 14

Vinson, Chief Justice Fred, 124
Virginia, State of
number of black voters prior to 1900, 17
opposition to ruling in *Smith v. Allwright*, 130
and racially biased limits on voter registration, 16
and vote denial, 18
Vote denial, 5
across nation, 8
and adoption of AWP, 20
and attack on AWP, 68
following Reconstruction, 14–15
in South, 8
Vote dilution, 15

{ *Index* }    155